To Be an Airline Pilot

12/25/09

Dear Brandth,
    follow your dreams!

        love,
    always
    Mom

To Be an Airline Pilot

Andrew Cook

Airlife

First published in 2006 by
Airlife Publishing, an imprint of
The Crowood Press Ltd
Ramsbury, Marlborough
Wiltshire SN8 2HR

www.crowood.com

This impression 2008

British Library Cataloguing-in-Publication Data
A catalogue record for this book is available from the British Library.

ISBN 978 1 86126 865 5

Typeset by SR Nova Pvt Ltd., Bangalore, India

Printed and bound in Spain by Graphycems.

CONTENTS

LIST OF ABBREVIATIONS

ADF	Automatic Direction Finding equipment	ISA	International Standard Atmosphere
AGK	Aircraft General Knowledge	JAA	Joint Aviation Authority
APU	Auxiliary Power Unit	JAR	Joint Aviation Requirements
ATC	Air Traffic Control	JOC	Jet Orientation Course
ATPL	Airline Transport Pilot's Licence	MEL	Minimum Equipment List
		METAR	Aerodrome weather report
BALPA	British Air Line Pilots Association	MCC	Multi-Crew Co-operation
		mb	Millibars, a measure of pressure
CAA	Civil Aviation Authority		
CAP	Civil Aviation Publication	NDB	Non-Directional Beacon
CAS	Calibrated Airspeed	NHP	Non-Handling Pilot
COAT	Corrected Outside Air Temperature	NOTAM	Notices To Airmen
		OBS	Omni Bearing Selector
CPL	Commercial Pilot's Licence	P2	Second pilot
DME	Distance Measuring Equipment	PIC	Pilot In Command
		POB	Persons On Board
EADI	Electronic Attitude Director Indicator	POF	Principles Of Flight
		PPL	Private Pilot's Licence
EAS	Equivalent Airspeed	PUT	Pilot Under Training
EFIS	Electronic Flight Instrument System	QFE	Aerodrome air pressure
		QFF	Mean sea-level pressure
EHSI	Electronic Horizontal Situation Indicator	QNH	Barometric pressure reduced to mean sea level
EICAS	Engine Indication and Crew Alerting System	QRH	Quick-Reference Handbook
ELT	Emergency Locator Transmitter	RNAV	Area Navigation
		RPM	Revolutions Per Minute
ETA	Estimated Time of Arrival	RT	Radiotelephony
FAA	Federal Aviation Administration	SEP	Safety Equipment and Procedures
FCL	Flight Crew Licensing	SID	Standard Instrument Departure
FCO	Flying Crew Orders		
FMS	Flight Management System	SIGMET	Significant Meteorological forecast
GAPAN	Guild of Air Pilots and Air Navigators	SOP	Standard Operating Procedure
GPS	Global Positioning System		
hPa	Hectopascal, a measure of pressure	SSR	Secondary Surveillance Radar
IAS	Indicated Airspeed	STAR	Standard Terminal Arrival Route
ICAO	International Civil Aviation Organization		
		TAF	Terminal Area Forecast
IFR	Instrument Flight Rules	TAS	True Airspeed
ILS	Instrument Landing System	TOW	Take-Off Weight
		VFR	Visual Flight Rules
IMC	Instrument Meteorological Conditions	VHF	Very High Frequency
		VOR	VHF Omni-directional Radio range
IR	Instrument Rating		

INTRODUCTION

When I was young, I would sit in the back garden of my family's home in Sussex, whether it was hot or cold, dry or wet, and watch the aircraft on their approach into Gatwick. At the airport, the smell of the fuel, the bustle of the people, the flow of aircraft around the apron and the roar of the engines were exciting and ignited the spark that has driven me since. No matter how you have caught the flying bug, I am sure that, like myself, you will settle for only one thing – a career in aviation.

I managed to talk my dad into paying for a trial flying lesson when I was fifteen, and it was a day that I will never forget. Initially, I was shocked at the small size of the aircraft, especially when my dad got in the back and ten minutes later we were pulling it out of the mud by its wings! Once settled, I forgot about everything except the task in hand, learning to fly. I didn't understand a single word that was said over the radio and I could not believe that we used a grass runway, but it was so peaceful and calm, the views were incredible and we were flying!

Flying is not cheap; I had one more flight and then it was around two-and-a-half years before I flew again. In the meantime, I studied for my A-Levels and tried to decide whether or not to go to university. I opted for a gap year, aiming to work and save enough money to obtain my PPL, and hoping that I would be successful in getting into a commercial pilot sponsorship scheme. I had a part-time job in a supermarket already, so I threw myself into it, working my way into a management position for the experience and extra money. At the age of eighteen, it takes a lot of effort to save money, especially when your mates are having nights out and buying cars, but perseverance and my passion for a flying career helped me stay focused. Within a year, I had the money I needed.

One day, while I was still saving hard and had just completed an application form for an airline pilot sponsorship, some terrorists flew aircraft into the twin towers of the World Trade Center in New York and the Pentagon in Washington. Like many, I was shocked and angry at the senseless acts, but I did not immediately realize the problems that they would cause for the airline industry. It did not take long, however, for pilot recruitment and pilot sponsorship schemes to cease, passenger numbers to crash, airlines to go bankrupt and pilots to lose their jobs around the world. It was a frustrating time, but even then I never thought of giving up.

Getting my PPL was a fantastic experience, which I will never forget. I chose to do an intensive course in Florida, and I had my licence within twenty-four days. It was hard work, but thoroughly enjoyable. There is nothing like getting up at sunrise, cycling in the early-morning heat to the airport and being airborne by 07.00, in the calm, warm air, with the golf courses, swamps and lakes of Florida spread out below, then landing at an airfield run by an old man in a rocking chair, who greets you with a cold drink. If I had had any doubts about my career choice, they would have vanished straight away.

When I returned home, the airline industry looked worse than ever, so I continued with my plan to go to university. I chose to study aerospace systems engineering at the University of Hertfordshire, and the work was more challenging than I expected, but the dream of getting on to the flight deck kept me going. In the meantime, I applied to join the University of London Air Squadron, successfully completing a stiff selection process – I am sure my passion for flying helped. The Air Squadron required a large amount of time and commitment, but this was worthwhile, and I benefited immensely from my membership. It was very enjoyable and I had some amazing flying experiences. I followed a structured flying schedule and flew sorties in general handling, spinning, aerobatics, formation flying and solo aerobatics, all of which were breathtaking experiences.

During my time at university, I applied for a commercial pilot sponsorship scheme, but I failed the aptitude test. I had done very well in my Royal Air Force aptitude test, so I think I may have just had a bad day, but I learned from the experience. I also applied for an ATPL scholarship from the Guild of Air Pilots and Air Navigators. In this, I was more successful. I found myself sitting more tests, but there were very few people in the room with me, so I assumed that other selection sessions were being held elsewhere. I was wrong, however, it was just us!

My adrenalin started pumping when I realized the great opportunity I had. I felt I did well in the tests, but after several agonizing days of waiting, I received a letter to say that I had not been chosen. However, GAPAN did want me and some of the other runners-up to meet with an airline and the flying school it employed to train pilots. The plan was for us to pay for the course ourselves and work together as a group, with support from GAPAN during training and when applying for jobs. I could not turn down this opportunity, joining four others to become the 'GAPAN 5'. One of our number soon won a part sponsorship with another airline, which left the 'GAPAN 4' preparing to train for our ATPLs in Jerez, Spain.

My reason for writing this book is because obtaining an ATPL is no small task. Spending so much money on the course cannot be taken lightly, and every aspect must be explored carefully. When I was trying to make my decision – looking into the training, the cost and necessary qualifications – I found it incredibly difficult to find answers to the many questions I had. When training, there are so many aspects that are challenging or confusing, and it is impossible to know what to expect. You can approach a flying school, but you will be talking to a salesperson, who will tell you what you want to hear, not necessarily what you need to hear. I hope that what you read here will answer many of the questions you may have before, during and after training for your ATPL.

This book is aimed at anybody who has shared my dream of becoming an airline pilot, or who is interested in what is achieved in the initial stages of airline pilot training. It is not intended as a textbook, but rather a guide to explain the hurdles you may face. I wrote it during my ATPL training, and it highlights the complications I encountered and enjoyment I experienced. I have also outlined what I did after the course and other options I explored to get into the industry.

I must emphasize that everything I have written has been from my personal viewpoint and experience. Before undertaking any training, conduct your own research into the risks and the content of any course. The information in this book is intended as a guide only and may not necessarily fit all of your particular circumstances or the training organization you choose.

ACKNOWLEDGEMENTS

The support I received from my family and friends during my ATPL course and the writing of this book was incredible, and I could not have completed either without it. So to them, I say thank you very much, especially to Hayley for putting up with me being away so much and for dealing with my stress over the phone!

Thanks also to Flight Training Europe, Jerez, Spain, for providing excellent training and allowing me to publish my experience of the training scheme; to the Guild of Air Pilots and Air Navigators for its advice and support throughout my training, with special thanks to Clive Elton; and to everyone on Course 39 for being great colleagues and great fun.

Chapter 1
What is the ATPL?

Understanding flying licences and their privileges can be quite complicated. Unfortunately, achieving your goal of becoming an airline pilot is not as simple as paying a fee and studying for the licence; there are many hurdles and difficulties to overcome before you can sit in the right-hand seat as second-in-command of a commercial aircraft. With persistence and a little careful planning, however, you can make the process easier, and the following chapters of this book should help you do that.

Every flying qualification comprises a basic licence, to which you can add 'ratings' that will allow you to expand the privileges of that licence, such as flying in low visibility and cloud – known as Instrument Meteorological Conditions (IMC). Among the flying licences you can obtain are:

- National Private Pilot's Licence (NPPL)
- Private Pilot's Licence (PPL)
- Commercial Pilot's Licence (CPL)
- Airline Transport Pilot's Licence (ATPL)

To all of these licences, except the NPPL, you can add the following ratings:

- Night Rating
- IMC Rating
- Instrument Rating
- Multi-Engine Rating
- Instructor's Rating

If you wanted to fly purely for recreational purposes and had no intention of obtaining a commercial qualification, an NPPL could be suitable. This licence restricts the holder to flight in basic lightweight aircraft in the UK and during the day only. Ratings can be added to the NPPL to match the type of aircraft you want to fly, such as Microlight, Self-Launching Motor Glider (SLMG) and Single-Engine Piston (SEP). The licence has lower medical requirements than other licences and does not require as much training as the PPL. The latter is also suitable as a recreational licence, but has much greater possibilities, allowing you to fly in Joint Aviation Authority (JAA) states during the day and offering a wider choice of ratings. It requires a Class 2 medical certificate. The PPL can be the first rung on the ladder to a commercial qualification. For this, you also need to obtain a CPL or ATPL.

A STEP-BY-STEP PROGRAMME

When training to become an airline pilot, typically you would go through a programme that consists of obtaining the following licences and ratings in the approximate order shown, depending on the training provider:

1. Private Pilot's Licence
2. Multi-Engine Rating
3. Night Rating
4. Commercial Pilot's Licence
5. Instrument Rating
6. Frozen Airline Transport Pilot's Licence
7. Type Rating

In most cases, your first flight right through to the Instrument Rating will be achieved at your flying school, resulting in the award of a Multi-Engine Commercial Pilot's Licence and Instrument Rating. These, along with passes in all of the ground-school exams, make up a frozen ATPL. If you are successful in gaining employment with an airline, the company will provide specific training on the aircraft you will fly so that you can gain the necessary type rating and begin to earn your keep.

TOWARD THE CAPTAIN'S SEAT

Of course, you may be dreaming of the ultimate goal – to become a captain. For this, you need to unfreeze your ATPL by amassing 1,500 hours of flying experience.

An ATPL for aircraft allows you to exercise all of the privileges of a PPL, a CPL and an Instrument Rating as the pilot in command or co-pilot of any aircraft type included on the licence. The minimum age for holding an ATPL is twenty-one years, and its period of validity is five years. Upon reaching sixty-five, the holder cannot pilot a public transport flight.

To obtain an ATPL, you will need:

- 1,500 hours of flight time (of which 100 hours can be gained on a simulator), including:
- 500 hours of multi-crew flight time
- 250 hours of pilot-in-command (PIC) time (of which 150 can be as pilot in command under supervision – PICUS)

- 200 hours of cross-country flight time (of which 100 must be as PIC or PICUS)
- 75 hours of instrument flight time (of which 30 hours can be instrument ground time)
- 100 hours of night flight time
- Passes in all fourteen ATPL theory examinations
- Completion of an approved Multi-Crew Co-operation course
- A pass in the ATPL skills test

So how long will it take to reach 1,500 hours? The most important task after you finish at the flying school is to obtain a type rating with an airline, and start flying as a co-pilot to build up your hours and experience. As a young first or second officer, you will probably fly about 900 hours a year. Given that you will already hold 200 hours or so, you can see that it will take only around one-and-a-half years to reach the 1,500 hours. Most airlines, however, will not be willing to promote you to captain until you have acquired sufficient experience, which may take as long as twelve years.

CHAPTER 2
WHEN TO TRAIN AND HOW TO FUND

Choosing a time to train is an important decision. You need to ensure that you are up to the task, that you are prepared financially and that the industry is ready for you. It may be that as much as you want to become a pilot, the job simply is not for you; there are ways of checking this for yourself. If you are certain that a career in flying is the right path to follow, then you need to maximize your chance of success.

APTITUDE TESTING

No matter what type of selection process you go through, at some point, it is likely that you will have to face a number of aptitude tests. In aviation, these are designed to demonstrate your ability to deal with problems, numbers, words, lateral thinking and, often, mechanical reasoning. There are psychometric tests as well, which are designed to give an insight into your personality. These are similar to the aptitude tests, but are easier and of greater variety. Rather than determining your aptitude, they place you into personality groups to indicate if you are the right kind of person for the job. There are many books and websites that give examples of such tests, allowing you to familiarize yourself with them, which can only be to the good when taking them for real.

Before committing yourself to any training, it would be of great benefit to know whether or not you do have the aptitude to be an airline pilot. This can be done by taking a test for real, which can be achieved in a number of ways. Many universities and higher-education centres run practice psychometric tests for those seeking employment. Although not aimed specifically at potential pilots, such tests will give you valuable experience in answering similar questions. I think the best way of ensuring that you have airline-pilot aptitude, however, is to take the aptitude test designed for Royal Air Force aircrew applicants. In 1996, the Guild of Air Pilots and Air Navigators negotiated with the RAF for the right to use its system, which since has been very successful. The scheme consists of a battery of tests that examine your co-ordination, memory, numeracy, verbal reasoning, and mechanical, planning and reaction skills. On completion, you are given your results and discuss your performance with a member of GAPAN, all of whom have a strong airline pilot training background. Although there is a charge for the tests, do not be put off by this, as it could prevent you from wasting a large amount of money if you are not a suitable candidate.

If you have already applied to join the RAF or have been in a University Air Squadron, you will have taken this test already and know if you met the requirements for a pilot. In this case, however, you will not have been given your score, as it is confidential to the RAF. If you reached the requirements for an RAF pilot, you would have achieved the score that GAPAN recommends for a good chance of success.

The following multiple-choice questions are similar to those I have faced in aptitude tests for various airlines, which will give you an idea of what to expect. Try to complete each question within fifteen seconds.

1) All employees should _____ from such a reward scheme.

   Result, Credit, Succeed, Enrol, Benefit?

2) What is 0.8 divided by 0.2?

   0.16, 0.25, 0.4, 4.0, 16.0

3) Which of the following lines is the odd one out?

   ----------   ----------   ----------   ----------   ----------

4) If 1500 balls cost £42.50, how much would 2500 cost?

   £25.50, £56.67, £70.83, £106.25, £78.80

5) What is 35.8 + 2.41?

   38.13, 33.39, 32.81, 33.11, 38.21

MEDICAL STANDARD

A possible setback for the potential airline pilot is his or her medical condition. The Civil Aviation Authority has differing requirements for private and commercial licences. If you are aiming to be an airline pilot, however, it is worth ensuring that you reach the correct medical standard from the outset. In fact, most training organizations will insist on this before you begin the course. A PPL requires a Class 2 medical certificate, but any commercial qualification requires a Class 1 certificate, which has many more criteria.

The initial Class 1 medical comprises many tests and is the most expensive. It is conducted at the UK CAA Aero Medical Centre at Gatwick Airport. As with aptitude testing, it is advisable to take the Class 1 medical before you spend time and money pursuing your career. Although you may feel well and healthy, and have no previous medical conditions, you may not meet the standard set by the CAA. This could be because you have a condition that does not affect everyday life or that shows no symptoms, but which may affect you when flying.

Your first Class 1 medical will take a few hours and consist of hearing and sight tests, a general examination, cholesterol and haemoglobin tests, a urine sample and chest X-ray. If you have any doubt about the quality of your eyesight, it may be worth seeking the advice of an optician before taking the Class 1. This could prevent any disappointment and save you the large cost of the medical.

The medical certificate needs revalidating every year, but subsequent medicals are less comprehensive and cost less. That said, since you are embarking on a career as an airline pilot, it is advisable to look after your body by maintaining a healthy diet and doing plenty of exercise from the outset. This could prevent troubles in the future and ease any concern about future medical certificate renewals.

START FLYING

If you have never had a flying lesson, yet you believe you were born to be an airline pilot, then the only way to be sure is to start flying. There are people who embark on airline pilot courses without ever having placed a foot in a light aircraft, but this has the potential to be a very costly mistake. Although flying lessons are expensive, an initial lesson is a priority. In addition to providing valuable experience, it will show future airline employers that you had the motivation to gain that experience before committing yourself to the career. It sounds even better if, to achieve your goal, you had to save every penny that you could earn from a paper round!

If a career in flying is for you, you will catch 'the bug' on your first flight. That first flight is something you will never forget, even after 5,000 hours on Jumbo jets. As you progress and gain more experience toward your first solo, things will get a little more difficult, and you will start to realize just how much work is required to be a pilot. Ideally, you should have flown solo before starting an integrated airline pilot's licence course. This will ensure that you have not only the ability, but also the confidence to be successful. You may find it a setback, however, if you begin an integrated course having gained many hours privately, as you are likely to have picked up bad flying habits that will be difficult to lose when trying to learn the way that your integrated school wants you to fly.

QUALIFICATIONS

Where qualifications for being an airline pilot are concerned, there really are no rules, but there are substantial differences in what people expect. Once, on a flight in a 747 to New York, I spoke to the captain on the flight deck and was surprised at his response when I asked him about qualifications. He told me that he had only managed to achieve five poor O-level results. That was some years ago, however, and today most airlines look for more academically gifted people. There are no requirements for the issue of an ATPL, but most employers specify a minimum of two science or mathematical based A levels at Grade C or above.

Some airlines prefer a university degree, while others are only concerned with your ability to fly aircraft. Having a degree allows you to further your knowledge toward a chosen career. A degree in aerospace engineering, for example, will give you valuable background knowledge for your ATPL exams. A degree also gives you something to fall back on if you cannot find employment in flying or if you ever lose your medical. That said, a degree in engineering would not allow you to become an engineer automatically, but it would make you more attractive to potential employers.

I had the opportunity to speak to the pilot recruitment manager of one of the biggest airlines in the world, and I put this issue to him. His response was that he did not look for potential pilots with degrees. He said that a degree was irrelevant and that if he were faced with two identical candidates for a job, one with a degree and one without, he would select the winning candidate based on flying experience and personality. Even so, my experience of a variety of airline sponsorship schemes is that the general trend is for successful candidates to have degrees.

The disadvantage of a degree is its cost in time and money. It takes around three years to get a degree; if you worked for that time instead, you could save a large amount toward the cost of your ATPL course. Studying for a degree also means that you will be three years older when you begin training for your licence. Obtaining an ATPL is not easy, and the younger you are, the easier it will be to learn the necessary skills. Also, a younger candidate is often at an advantage in an interview, although this does vary from one airline to another.

So work hard to achieve the best possible grades at A level. That is what most airlines will look for when you apply for employment. If you are considering going to university first, seek the advice of airlines, weigh up the pros and cons, then decide what is best for you.

YOUR AGE

As with qualifications, age is a controversial topic, with many differing views throughout the industry.

> He shall not fly such an aeroplane on a flight for the purpose of public transport after he attains the age of 60 years unless the aeroplane is fitted with dual controls and carries a second pilot who has not attained the age of 60 years and who holds an appropriate licence under this Order entitling him to act as pilot in command or co-pilot of that aeroplane. (*LASORS* – the CAA's guide to safety and licensing)

He shall not at any time after he attains the age of 65 years act as pilot in command or co-pilot of any aeroplane on a flight for the purpose of public transport. (*LASORS*)

As well as the maximum age restrictions quoted above, an applicant for a Commercial Pilot's Licence or a frozen ATPL must be at least eighteen years old, while an unfrozen ATPL cannot be gained until the applicant is twenty-one years old.

Generally speaking, the younger you are when applying for a job with an airline, the better your chances. It takes a lot of money to train someone on an aircraft type, and companies prefer young pilots so that they can get a return on this outlay. That said, some airlines do not like to recruit young applicants because of maturity issues. At least one will not consider applicants under the age of twenty-nine.

Another age consideration that you should face is your ability to learn new things as you grow older. Statistics from flight training schools clearly indicate that students in their early twenties tend to achieve better results and more first-time passes than older students. Again, this does depend on individual circumstances. If you are in your thirties or forties, do not be put off training for an airline career, but be honest with yourself and take the aptitude tests first to ensure that your are still capable of picking up new things quickly.

WHEN TO TRAIN?

Timing is crucial. In the modern airline industry, however, it is very difficult to make an accurate forecast of employment prospects. One of the most useful guides in deciding when to train is to listen to what the airlines are saying. Obviously, they will not contact you and tell you that they are thinking of recruiting; you need to chase after them. Most airline websites will have 'recruitment' sections that will tell you a company's current employment status. Websites can be unreliable, though, because they may not be updated regularly, so find other ways. You can write to companies, email them and contact them by telephone, but the way to achieve the best results is to go and see them. Although you may feel that you are being a nuisance by turning up at an airline's head office and asking if the company is recruiting, you may get to talk to the relevant person rather than an administration assistant. While you are there, you can ask other questions about the company's requirements and so on.

Study newspapers and aviation magazines for any clues. A trend I have noticed is that when the largest companies start to recruit, the smaller ones follow suit. If you see that the larger airlines are making bigger profits, that could be an excellent indicator. Look for anything else that may be a positive sign toward recruitment, such as strike action by overworked pilots and new airlines starting up. Do not make the mistake of waiting until the airlines actually begin recruiting. Remember that an integrated ATPL course will take around fourteen months; by the time you are qualified, the airlines are likely to have taken on a huge number of new recruits and will be easing off again. By attempting to predict the recruitment trend using the methods described, at least you should be able to reduce the risk of missing an employment boom completely.

Due to acts of terrorism, war and natural disasters, the airline industry is somewhat unstable. If incidents such as those that took place on 11 September 2001 or the Gulf War of the early nineties occur, they will have a devastating effect on the industry. When the former terrorist attacks took place, I was going through the process of applying for airline sponsorship and saving money so that I could pay for a course myself if needed. As the events of that day unfolded, I had no idea of the extent to which the industry would be affected. One of the problems with this kind of incident is that it is completely unpredictable and, in my opinion, it should not play a part in the decision-making process. If you take war and terrorism into account, you will find great difficulty in ever training, because there is always a risk. Airlines have become much more tolerant of disasters since 2001. Due to the rationalization and cost-cutting exercises carried out by all airlines in the early part of the twenty-first century, the industry is in much better shape to deal with future catastrophes. Most have emergency plans and are operating much more efficiently than before. So if there is an industry crash again, recovery should be quicker.

A final factor that should be mentioned is that no other method of transport competes with commercial aviation. There is no other way of crossing the Atlantic or reaching the other side of the world in just a few hours. Air transport is essential and will remain so for the foreseeable future, and as long as that is the case, airline pilots will be required.

FUNDING YOUR TRAINING

There are several ways of funding your training, each having advantages and disadvantages. Occasionally, airlines offer sponsorships; scholarships may also be available. You can 'pay as you go' and do the training over a number of years while working simultaneously to fund it, or you could consider a career development loan.

Sponsorship

In the nineties, airline sponsorship was the primary method of becoming a commercial pilot. There were lots of opportunities, and the airlines were more than willing to fund them. In the modern airline industry, however, where operating budgets are much lower following a number of years of cost cutting, this is no longer an option for most companies. While some airlines do occasionally run sponsorship schemes, they do not cover the full training costs, and they require a huge commitment on your part toward the airline involved. With fewer schemes on offer, the ratio of applicants to the number of opportunities is high. As a result, the age, academic and financial requirements are much tighter.

Increasingly, airlines are offering schemes whereby you can become 'approved' by sitting the selection process before taking an integrated flying training course. This gives you an excellent opportunity, but there are no guarantees, and you may still have to pay for the integrated course yourself.

Airline sponsorships and 'approved' schemes are advertised in aviation magazines, on airline websites and on the BALPA website (BALPA membership is free for student pilots).

When you have found a scheme that suits you, it is likely that you will take part in a selection process. Most of the selection procedure is discussed later in this book, but for the initial application, there are some important considerations:

- Spelling and grammar should be immaculate. This is a very easy way for a sponsor to filter out thousands of applications; many chief airline pilots have confirmed this. Do not let yours be one of those applications.
- Do not lie about anything.
- Answer the question asked, not the question you wish you were answering.
- Make sure you meet the basic requirements.

The usual steps for selection appear to be:

1. Application
2. Aptitude
3. Group exercises
4. Interview

This may vary in detail from one airline to another.

Scholarships

Sometimes, scholarships are offered for specific aspects of flying, such as PPL, Flying Instructor, Jet Orientation Course or even a fully integrated frozen ATPL.

The Guild of Air Pilots and Air Navigators, for example, has offered one fully integrated 'J.N. Somers' ATPL scholarship each year, but naturally the selection process has been tough. Past requirements for applicants have included holding a PPL and a Class 1 medical certificate, although these have often been relaxed. Suitable candidates would be asked to attend psychometric testing, an aptitude test and an interview. Then the successful applicant would be placed at a flying school of the Guild's choice.

Self-Finance

Taking a self-financed modular route would enable you to spread the cost of training by taking time off between modules to work and save for the next part of the course. This does take a lot of time, however, and there is less continuity in the training, so the outcome may be poorer. You may even require more training, adding to the cost.

Another method is simply to save for the course over a number of years. It would take a long time to amass the funds for a complete integrated course, unless you had a high salary, but to reduce the time, you could save part of the cost and take out a bank loan for the remainder. A bank is more likely to offer a professional studies loan if it can see that you have already saved for part of the cost.

Some banks offer career development loans, which could cover the complete cost of an integrated flying course and associated expenses. Such loans can be hard to come by, however, and you need to put a good case to the bank manager. I funded my training by this method, and my advice is to show the manager plenty of evidence of your commitment, together with any aptitude tests that you have passed; a recommendation letter from GAPAN aptitude testing would be an excellent asset. Assemble a case that the manager will find difficult to fault, take copies of pilot recruitment advertisements from magazines or printouts from the Internet, even draw up a graph of the increasing number of pilot vacancies that you have counted in the previous few months (if this is the case).

A guarantor may be required for this type of loan. That means someone who is prepared to sign a legally binding agreement that they will meet any repayments you do not make. One big disadvantage of funding a course by this method is the extra cost due to interest, which could be in the region of 30 per cent of the price of the course. If you do have a small income, you may be able to make the interest payments as they are charged, rather than having them added to your loan during your training. This will save a little money, as it avoids paying interest on the interest!

Before taking out such a large loan, you should consider the problem of failing to obtain a flying career at the end of your training. Be realistic, could you really afford the repayments? Normally, interest rates on this kind of loan are variable, so you need to consider the effect of an increase in interest rate; could you still afford the repayments if the interest rate tripled or quadrupled?

If, after presenting your case to the bank manager, the answer is negative, try asking your chosen flying school for help. It is in the school's interest to help you, and you may find that it will inform the bank of your successful selection or confirm the demand for pilots. You can also ask the school if previous students have obtained professional studies loans and, if so, ask for a contact name. On your visit to the school, chat to current students, as they may be able to help you with banking contacts or give you advice on obtaining a loan.

In finding funds for your course, as with all aspects of obtaining a career in aviation, networking is often the key.

CHAPTER 3
WHERE TO TRAIN

Choosing the training provider for your course is one of the most important decisions that you will make. It can have a significant effect on your future career prospects, as many schools have links with particular airlines. Some airlines only recognize certain flying schools, so you will need to research this very carefully to find a school that matches your aspirations. Just like buying a car, it is important to shop around to make sure that you get the best deal and exactly what you are looking for. You can start compiling a list of potential training providers from the following sources:

- The Internet
- Flying magazines
- Flying exhibitions
- BALPA employment conferences
- The Guild of Air Pilots and Air Navigators, London
- Individual airlines – ask if they recognize particular schools

When you have assembled a list of schools, you need to research them all by obtaining their prospectuses and asking them pertinent questions (*see* box).

Questions to Ask Training Schools

- How many people from the last three courses are now employed as pilots with airlines?
- What other costs may I have to pay for outside the integrated package?
- What happens to the accommodation costs if the course overruns due to bad weather, aircraft technical problems etc?
- If I fail a test, how much will the extra flying and exams cost?
- How many instructors do you have per student?
- What is the first-time pass rate for your Instrument Rating tests?
- What is the average ground-school mark at your flying school?
- Can I pay for my training in instalments?
- With which airlines are you in contact, and to which have you provided pilots?
- What is the weather like here?
- How many aircraft are there per student?

I would advise avoiding the kind of school that advertises 'bargain' ATPLs or guarantees a job at the end of the course – it's just not possible. It is well worth visiting a few of the schools too; even if a school is overseas, the relatively small cost of making a visit at this stage could prevent you from wasting a lot of money later at an establishment that provides poor training.

WHAT TO LOOK FOR

When you visit a school, you need to make the most of your time there. The most valuable outcome of a visit is being able to talk to current students, perhaps in the bar, where you will learn the truth about the school, whether it is good or bad. Remember, though, that all schools will have their drawbacks, and bear in mind to whom you are talking. Someone who has just graduated with flying colours, for example, will probably give a much more positive opinion than a student who has had a bad day and failed a test. Talking to the students will also suggest a lot of questions to ask the flying school.

Take a good look around the campus. Check that the classrooms are big enough and well equipped; do they have heating and/or air conditioning? Take a good look at the operations department. Does it seem to be organized and running smoothly; does it have all the equipment you need for flying? Make sure that the simulators are in good condition and of good quality; check to see if they have air conditioning too. Take a good look at the aircraft. They should appear in good condition. The engineering department is always a good place to visit. If it is large and well-staffed, there should be a good chance of the aircraft being available when you need them.

Then you need to inspect the other facilities, such as accommodation. Are the bedrooms big and clean; do they have an en-suite facilities? You will be spending a lot of time in your room and will need a good environment for studying. You will also need facilities for washing, drying and ironing clothes. The dining-room, bar and leisure facilities should also be checked, as should transport links to a nearby town and supermarket. Visiting a school will really give you a good feel for the environment and people, especially if you can spend a night there. I visited my training school twice before I started the course, spending two nights there. It was well worth doing, allowing me to make friends before I began in earnest.

CONSIDER THE COST

The course fee charged by a school is also a factor to consider, but I believe it is of minor importance. Gaining employment in such a sought-after job is tough at the best of times; if you restrict the quality of your training because of cost, it will only make your search for a position harder. Usually, the schools that provide the best training and offer the best chance of getting a job quickly are more expensive than schools that use cheap aircraft and do not have any links with airlines.

It is essential to check that the price quoted really is for an integrated course; often, there will be hidden costs, such as exam fees. You need to ask if there are any other costs too, so that you can budget for them. Even something as minor as having to pay for tea and coffee in the crew room can make a significant difference to your outlay.

Some hidden costs to look for are:

- Fuel surcharges if the price of fuel rises
- Landing fees
- Food
- Refuelling when flying solo to other airports
- Medical renewal
- Licence application fee
- Graduation costs
- Uniform
- Stationery for ground school
- Refreshments between meals (tea, coffee)
- Equipment, such as a flight bag and plotter

LOCATION, LOCATION

The final factor to consider when choosing a school is its location. You could train within easy reach of your home, go farther afield for a residential course or even go overseas. The advantage of training near where you live is that you could save costs by staying at home. That is likely to incur travelling costs to and from the airport each day, however, and you would have to

Training abroad has obvious benefits, but beware of the drawbacks too!

consider whether or not you would be distracted from studying. Opting for a residential course some distance from home is a good option, in that it allows you to put all of your concentration into studying, but you can still go home occasionally if you want.

I believe that studying abroad has many benefits too. There is a good chance that the weather would be better, so the flying schedule is less likely to be interrupted; the cost of living can be cheaper; and there are no distractions from home to affect your studies. However, there are disadvantages too: you may have to factor in extra costs for a few flights home; there may be a language barrier; the exchange rate could change during your training, altering the cost; and when you return to the UK, you will not be so familiar with the airspace. If you have a partner, being away from him or her for such a long period could have an adverse effect on you, your training and your relationship. It may seem like a great idea to go to some fantastic destination abroad for over a year, but remember, it will be nothing like a holiday!

MAKE UP YOUR OWN MIND

When you are investigating flying schools, make sure you do your own research and lots of it. The schools can provide lots of statistics, help and advice, but you must bear in mind that they are selling a product and want your money. They will do anything to get you to sign on the dotted line, so be absolutely certain in your own mind that you are doing the right thing.

CHAPTER 4
THE COURSE
STRUCTURE

The structure of the ATPL course will vary considerably from school to school, each format having advantages and disadvantages. Due to JAA regulations, however, all courses will be based on the same requirements, so they should have the basic layout in common.

A modular course differs from an integrated course, as do the JAA requirements. If you opt for a modular course, you will have to organize your own training and complete the various stages at your own convenience. Such a course may be broken down into around five stages. Although I will concentrate on the integrated course structure, as that was how I studied, I have included a guide to modular courses. Bear in mind, however, that the structure can be varied depending on your requirements.

A TYPICAL MODULAR COURSE

Stage 1: PPL. Obtaining your PPL is the first hurdle to consider as a modular student. A PPL requires forty-five hours of flight training and some ground-school exams.

Stage 2: ATPL ground school. All the ATPL theoretical exams must be completed to obtain a Commercial Pilot's Licence. You will be allowed a number of sittings for the fourteen exams and will be able to retake any that you fail.

Stage 3: Hour building. Before being able to take a CPL skills test and gaining your licence, you will need to obtain the necessary proficiency and experience. This is done by 'hours building'. Often, the best way of doing this is to buy a package of flying hours at a discounted rate. You will also need to obtain your Night Rating by flying five hours at night, your Multi-Engine Rating and some instrument flying experience.

Stage 4: CPL and IR. This stage is probably the most critical. It is a course of intensive training that will provide you with the necessary skills to pass your Commercial Pilot's Licence and Instrument Rating skills tests. You will need around twenty-five hours of CPL training and fifty hours of instrument flying training. Many flying schools offer this stage of your training as an intensive training package.

Stage 5: Multi-Crew Co-operation. As with an integrated course, to gain a type rating with an airline, you will need to have an MCC certificate. This is obtained through a twenty-hour flight-simulator course (*see* Chapter 9).

A TYPICAL INTEGRATED ATPL COURSE STRUCTURE

The breakdown of the structure used at the school where I studied was as follows.

Weeks 1–19 (Phase One) – Full-time ground school.
    Studying – AGK
          – Meteorology
          – General Navigation
          – Radio Navigation
          – Mass and Balance
          – Principles of Flight

Week 20 – JAA exams for above subjects.

Weeks 21–43 (Phase Two) – Single-engine integrated training with Phase Two ground school.
    Studying – Performance
          – Instruments
          – Human Performance and Limitations
          – Aviation Law and ATC Procedures
          – Operational Procedures
          – Flight Planning and Monitoring
          – VFR Communications
          – IFR Communications

Week 44 – JAA exams for above subjects.

Weeks 45–57 – Complex flying training (twin-engine).

Weeks 58–60 – Multi-crew co-operation.

Holidays – four days at Easter and two weeks at Christmas.

Phase One

At most training establishments, the first part of the course will be full-time ground school. There is a very large amount of studying to do on the ground, and the best approach is to complete a lot of it before you start flying. This ensures that you have the basic knowledge of the various aspects of flying and have time to concentrate on flying, rather than having all the exams to worry

In the second phase, the flying lessons will help to reinforce your ground-school studies, such as the use of Air Traffic Control and airport laws.

about at the same time. Completing six of the largest subjects is a great boost to morale. Subject to passing the exams, flying starts the following week. If you do not pass all the exams, you will need to retake any you have failed as soon as possible. Subject to the school's policy, however, if you have to resit more than two exams, you may need to go back to a previous course to have the time to study – this will cost you time and money.

Phase Two

Once the celebrations of passing the first phase have finished, Phase Two begins. The workload will rapidly increase for the last eight JAA exams, and for the flying that soon becomes a challenge, requiring even more time spent studying on the ground than spent in the air. Around half-way into this phase, there is a flying test, which is equivalent to that for a Private Pilot's Licence, but to a higher standard.

The six months that make up Phase Two are structured so that flying and ground school are alternated on a daily basis. This seems to work well, as the flying keeps you enthused, and let's face it, that is why you are on the training course. The ground school allows the lessons learned from the flying to sink in, and for you to take a breather after an exhausting day in the air. That said, after a long day of flying, it is difficult to find the energy to study on the ground the next day! The Phase Two subjects link in with your flying training nicely, and vice versa, in areas such as Flight Planning, Air Law and Performance.

Complex flying training

After around five months of this integrated period, you sit the Phase Two exams. Upon passing them, you should be at the stage of moving on to flying twin-engined aircraft. From then on, the flying becomes full time, and you should almost be ready to take the Commercial Pilot's Licence (CPL) flying test. After you have gained your CPL, the main focus of all the remaining time in the air is on instrument flying, as the Instrument Rating test occurs between six and eight weeks after the CPL test.

Multi-crew co-operation

With the Instrument Rating test under your belt, the MCC course starts. At the beginning, this consists of a lot of classroom work, studying MCC scenarios and problems, followed by sixteen hours of multi-crew flying in a jet simulator. By now, the end of the course is approaching and the next phase is to prepare your CV.

A FLEXIBLE STRUCTURE

You must bear in mind that the school's job is to provide you with the necessary training for a frozen ATPL, and the course structure that it gives you is likely to be an outline only. Depending on student numbers, the weather and the school's situation, it is possible that the structure will change to suit immediate needs, so don't be surprised if you spend longer in full-time ground school than anticipated. Check your contract.

Chapter 5
Ground School – Phase One

In this chapter, I will include some personal experiences from the first phase of my course and discuss the subjects that were studied. I will also give some personal tips and practicalities of the subjects, together with my account of the JAA exams. Bear in mind that the content of the various course phases will vary from one school to another, so the subjects I studied in Phase One may not be covered in the same order by a different school.

It was with some trepidation that I packed my things and made my way to the flying school in Spain. I knew there was no going back, my debt would be huge, I would be away from loved ones for a very long time, and I had little idea of what I would be going though over the following fifteen months. I was fortunate to be travelling to the school and starting the course with a friend; since we had similar concerns, we could talk them over together.

Although I had already visited the school twice before, so there were no surprises, it was a very strange feeling to move my things into new accommodation and experience new surroundings with new people. I met the other students on my course that evening, and the early signs were very promising. It was good to get to know them in a relaxed atmosphere before the classroom work started. It made the first few days much easier.

The first working day was made up of introductions, administration and welcome talks from the various departments and management. It was all very organized and proved an excellent opportunity to get to know both students and staff better, to discover how the ATPL course was broken down, and to gain some information about the local area – where to shop, eat, find leisure facilities and so on.

The course began officially on the following Monday and consisted mainly of introductions from the various instructors. In all the subjects, we started the syllabus by looking at the basics. In fact, the first few days were better than I expected, as the lessons were introduced gently, and nothing was too demanding. That changed very quickly, however, and soon I began to realize the amount of work that was required of me. The beginning of the course went well, a lot of it being revision of the PPL work that I had done previously (for example pressure instruments, navigation computer, piston engines, simple electronics and basic meteorology). The reality of being away from home, the cost of the training and the employment prospects had really hit me, however, and I found the evenings, when I was not too busy, very difficult because of these concerns. In such circumstances, I would advise you to write a list of all the positive reasons for doing the course, so that you can look at it from time to time to remind yourself that you have made the correct decision.

The following pages provide an individual breakdown of each subject in Phase One, my thoughts and experiences of the subject, helpful tips and exam techniques, plus any other relevant details.

AIRCRAFT GENERAL KNOWLEDGE (AGK)

AGK comprises three main components:

1. Aircraft Systems
2. Electrics
3. Engines

Although I studied the components individually, the final JAA exam covered all three in one paper. Some schools may study them as an integrated subject. Aircraft systems, engines and electrics vary considerably from one aircraft to another, so the JAA has standardized the aircraft for study purposes, settling on the Boeing 737-400.

Aircraft Systems

The subject of Aircraft Systems is broken down further into a number of sub-divisions (again, this may vary from one school to another):

- Aircraft Structures
- Hydraulics
- Flying Controls
- Gears, Wheels and Brakes
- Air Conditioning and Pressurization
- Fuel Systems
- Ice Protection
- Fire and Emergency

Aircraft Structures

Although there are many different types of aircraft, most have similar components, and this subject will give you a good understanding of the main points. For the exams, it is important to have a good appreciation of the types of stresses and loads on the aircraft structure, and how they are absorbed. Throughout your training, this will continue to appear, mainly in the POF syllabus.

Aircraft Structures Sample Questions

1) In the context of airframe load path philosophies, what is a fail-safe component?
2) The fuselage of an aircraft consists of stringers, among others, what is their purpose?
3) On a non-stressed-skin-type wing, the wing structure elements that take up the vertical bending moments Mx are?
4) What is the purpose of the wing ribs?
5) What is control-surface flutter and which two types of stress cause it?
6) What are flight-deck windows made from?
7) What is a torsion box?

Hydraulics

You will learn about the characteristics of various hydraulic systems, problems and valves. It is important to understand the basic energy concepts; a knowledge of Newton's laws is vital throughout the whole ATPL syllabus.

I found that the most commonly asked questions in the exam concerned aircraft structures, hydraulics, flying controls and air conditioning. Although there may be some questions on fire and emergencies, these subjects tended to be covered in the Operational Procedures syllabus. As you will see in the

---

Hydraulics Sample Questions

1) What hydraulic fluid is found in the 737-400?
2) What is the usual pressure in a hydraulic system?
3) What is the colour of synthetic hydraulic oil?
4) What is the purpose of a hand pump on a hydraulic system?
5) What is the name of the component that transforms hydraulic pressure into a linear motion?
6) In which component of a hydraulic system would the overheat indicators be found?
7) What is the purpose of an accumulator?
8) What does low gas pressure in an accumulator cause?
9) What is a stoppage in a fuel feeding line caused by a fuel vapour bubble known as?
10) What is the purpose of a relief valve?
11) What type of hydraulic fluid has the highest resistance against cavitation?
12) Hydraulic fluids must have which of the following characteristics?
    a) Thermal stability
    b) Corrosion resistance
    c) High viscosity
    d) Good resistance to combustion
    e) Low emulsifying characteristics
    f) High compressibility
    g) High volatility

---

sample questions about hydraulics on page 31, many of the questions are simple and factual.

Flying Controls

The subject of flying controls crops up regularly throughout the ATPL syllabus, so a good understanding will pay dividends. In AGK, however, you may be asked questions on powered flying controls, which ties in with the hydraulics section. Generic aircraft systems are studied, including the trimming system, the EICAS (Engine Indicating and Crew Alerting System) and spoilers. Where the last are concerned, you need to know how they can be used to assist the ailerons, and act as speed brakes or lift dumpers. Also, you must understand how the spoilers are operated from within the flight deck and some of the problems associated with the control systems. Perhaps the most common questions from the flying controls section, however, will be concerned with what happens to the control surfaces and their associated trim tabs if the flying controls are turned to port, pulled aft etc.

Flying Controls Sample Questions

1) Where are Kreuger flaps positioned?
2) What is the purpose of trim tabs?
3) Why does the trim switch on a control column consist of two separate switches?
4) Why are flaps and slats used? (In terms of lift and drag.)
5) What are the benefits of cabled controls?
6) If the rudder control is moved right, the right aileron up and the left aileron down, what will happen to the aircraft's attitude?
7) Why is a yaw damper fitted?

Gears, Wheels and Brakes

When studying the components of landing gears, your knowledge of hydraulics will come in handy for understanding retraction and extension

---

Gears, Wheels and Brakes Sample Questions

1) What is the purpose of the torque links in a landing-gear leg?
2) What is the type of brake unit found on most modern transport aircraft?
3) How may nose-wheel shimmy be described?
4) What is the purpose of the oil in an oleo-pneumatic strut?
5) What lights are shown on the flight deck to indicate that the landing gear is locked down?
6) Where are thermal plugs found and what is their purpose?
7) In case of failure of the main landing-gear lowering system, how could the landing gear be lowered?

A typical wheel and brake assembly for a jet aircraft.

systems. The braking-system (single- and multi-disc) components and characteristics are covered, as well as auto brakes and anti-skid. The last is important, as it will be included in the Performance and possibly Operation Procedures syllabuses.

Air Conditioning and Pressurization
I found air conditioning and pressurization systems to be complex subjects. There are several different types of system, and you will need to know all of them and their principles of operation. Even the most fundamental aspect of an air conditioning system must be known, which is the quantity of air required for each passenger to breathe, and at what temperature and relative humidity it should be delivered (Meteorology syllabus).

The three types of air conditioning system studied are ram air, air-cycle cooling (also known as bootstrap) and vapour-cycle cooling. I found that the exam questions were framed such that all you needed to know for each system was the path of components through which the air travels (in the correct order) and a very basic understanding of what each component does to the air (in terms of its temperature and pressure).

Also covered in this section are the types of decompression, and naturally this leads on to the physiological effects of altitude and supplemental oxygen systems. You will find that this is also covered in the Human Performance and Limitations syllabus. The different types of oxygen system (continuous flow, diluter demand and portable oxygen) should be understood and their components known. Chemical oxygen generator systems are important too, as they are most commonly used for passengers in modern aircraft. Oxygen masks for flight crew and cabin crew should be studied as well. All of these oxygen requirements and systems are very important; it is not uncommon to find four or five related questions in the Operational Procedures exam.

Air Conditioning and Pressurization Sample Questions

1) Define 'conditioned air'.
2) What is the purpose of a ditching control switch?
3) In a cabin air conditioning system, equipped with a bootstrap, the mass air flow is routed via what?
4) Which component regulates cabin pressure?
5) During cruise flight with air conditioning packs on, the outflow valve closes. What happens to the pressure differential?
6) What is the maximum normal cabin altitude?
7) What is the maximum differential pressure in a large transport aircraft?
8) Between what components is the water separator fitted?
9) At what altitude is a quick donning oxygen mask required for flight crew?
10) What happens to the differential pressure as an aircraft climbs?

Fuel Systems

Fuel comes in many types. Knowing the colours of the different fuels, what they are used for, contamination problems, possible additives and a little about their content is sufficient for the exam. A large fuel system will be studied, probably that of the generic 737-400, and you will learn how the fuel is transferred from tank to tank, how it is delivered to the engines, the back-up systems, the different types of valve, the fuel pressurization system, how the fuel pumps are cooled, how air is kept out of the system and so on. You should be familiar with schematic diagrams, as one may be used in an exam question concerning the method of cross-feeding fuel.

Fuel Systems Sample Questions

1) If a fuel sample appears cloudy and it clears slowly from the top, what does this indicate?
2) When is a fuel dumping system required?
3) What type of pump is a booster pump?
4) What is the purpose of a vent in a fuel system?
5) How much vent space is required in a fuel tank according to JAR 23 and JAR 25?
6) What voltage is supplied to booster pumps on a modern jet airliner?
7) The octane rating of a fuel characterizes what?
8) What is the function of a feeder box in a twin-jet fuel system?

Ice Protection

For icing, an understanding of the methods of preventing or removing ice (pneumatic boots) is important, including a basic knowledge of de-icing fluids, as questions about these may also occur in Operational Procedures. Ice detection is in the syllabus too, and this will cover such methods as vibrating rods, hot rod detector head and serrated rotor detectors.

Ice Protection Sample Questions

1) On modern transport aircraft, how are flight-deck windows protected against icing?
2) When is windscreen heating activated?
3) On a modern turbo-prop aircraft, what is the method of de-icing the wing?
4) In a bleed-air anti-icing system, which areas are heated?
5) How much ice build-up (cm) is required to be able to operate the pneumatic boots?

Fire and Emergency

It is essential to have an excellent understanding of fire, as questions will be asked in both AGK and Operational Procedures. Knowing the type of extinguishers to be used on each type of fire is important and can be remembered relatively easily.

Smoke detectors are also covered in some detail, both the resistive and capacitive type. Fire extinguishers in the wheel bays, engines and APU are studied. You should have an understanding of how these work, how the engine fire-extinguisher cross-feed system operates, how all these systems are tested and their potential faults.

Although it is possible that you may be asked about emergency equipment, that is not very likely in this exam. However, it will crop up in the Operational Procedures exam (*see* Chapter 6).

Fire and Emergency Sample Questions

1) What is the best extinguisher for a wheel fire?
2) What should be used on a magnesium fire?
3) In which compartments are smoke detectors fitted?
4) Continuous-loop fire detector systems operate on the principle that an increase in temperature causes what change to resistance?
5) How are fire wire detection systems tested?
6) What is the warning on the flight deck if a fire detection system activates?
7) Why does a bimetallic fire detection system have an inbuilt delay?
8) What are the fire precautions to be observed before refuelling?

Electrics

The subject of electrics does not form a large part of the AGK exam; most questions are about engines and systems. When I took the exam, the questions were about the basics of the theory. I found studying electrics to be a challenge, and I wasn't the only student on my course to hold that view, but perseverance paid off. I think it is very important to be confident about each aspect of the subject before going on to the next, as each part builds on the previous one. Electrics is broken down into the following subject areas:

- Basic Direct Current (DC) Theory
- Aircraft Wiring and Circuit Protection
- Batteries
- Magnetism
- DC Generators and DC Motors
- Inductance, Capacitance and AC (Alternating Current) Theory
- Three-Phase Electrics
- Semiconductors
- Logic Circuits and Computing

Basic Direct Current Theory
This covers all the basics of electrics that would have been taught in physics at school. You will learn about the construction of atoms, laws of electrical charge, conductors and insulators, and how a basic electrical circuit works. It is important to know the formulae for Ohm's Law, Kirchoff's Law etc. It is unlikely that you will be asked any calculation questions in the exams, however, just to state the relationships between the variables.

Basic Direct Current Theory Sample Questions

1) In what units is electrical potential rated?
2) State Ohm's Law.
3) For what can a Wheatstone bridge circuit be used?
4) In what units is resistance rated?

Aircraft Wiring and Circuit Protection
This aspect of electrics concerns circuit faults and the protection devices used, together with the problems of static electricity. There are various types of fuse, current limiter and circuit breaker, and they all need to be known. If static electricity is not removed from an aircraft, it can cause many problems. There are several methods of removal, all of which are studied.

Aircraft Wiring and Circuit Protection Sample Questions

1) In what units is a fuse rated?
2) How can you tell when bonding is incorrect?
3) What are the advantages of a dipole system?
4) What is the purpose of static discharge wicks?
5) What is the purpose of bonding?

Batteries
All aircraft systems include a battery, so it is important to learn about them. You will need to know all the components of a battery and their functions,

---

Batteries Sample Questions

1) What are the advantages of NICAD batteries?
2) What is the voltage of a fully charged lead-acid battery?
3) What would be the effect if one of the twelve cells of a lead-acid battery became broken?
4) How would you test the charge of a lead-acid battery?
5) How is the capacity of a battery expressed?

---

such as the electrolyte, the plates and the terminals. Also, you should understand how batteries are rated and connected (in series or parallel). Two types of battery should be studied: the lead-acid and the alkaline (nickel-cadmium – NICAD) battery. It is important to know what types of aircraft would use these and why.

Magnetism
A knowledge of the basics of magnetism is essential, such as electron fields, electromagnetic fields and the laws of magnetism. An understanding of relevant materials is also desirable, such as hard and soft iron, and the meaning of ferro-, para- and dia-magnetism. The 'right-hand grasp rule' and 'Fleming's right-hand rule for generators' often crop up in this subject and can create easy marks in your exam. In this section, the principles of electromagnets and solenoids are introduced; it is important to have a clear understanding of these concepts, as many aircraft systems contain relays that work on the solenoid principle.

Magnetism Sample Questions

1) What is a relay?
2) What happens when a conductor cuts the flux of a magnetic field?
3) What is a solenoid?
4) Why is a relay used?

DC Generators and DC Motors
It is essential to understand the theory behind DC generators and motors. The components of a very basic DC generator (yoke, armature, quill drive, brushes etc.) must all be known and understood, as well as the principle of operation of both DC generators and motors. The theory of and reasons for using shunt-wound, series-wound or compound-wound generators and motors are often examined. Voltage regulators are important parts of generators, and you must know how they work, what they do and what types are available.

Once you have an understanding of DC generators, motors, batteries, loads and relays, it is easier to understand electrical circuit diagrams. Differential

---

DC Generators and DC Motors Sample Questions

1) How is the voltage regulator of a DC generator connected?
2) How is load sharing achieved when two DC generators are operating in parallel?
3) What is necessary to ensure that DC generators will achieve equal load sharing when operating in parallel?
4) If the load increases on a constant-speed generator, what does the voltage regulator do?
5) What conditions are necessary for DC generators to operate in parallel?
6) What is a static inverter?
7) Do shunt-wound DC motors have a low or high starting torque, and should they be started on or off load?

---

cut-out and reverse-current circuit breakers are used to protect electrical circuits, and will be covered in depth. In twin-engine aircraft, there may be two DC generators, creating larger, more complicated circuits. To decipher these larger circuits, an understanding of busbars and load sharing is necessary. Some time is spent studying this type of circuit and the implications of operating DC generators in parallel.

Inductance, Capacitance and AC Theory
If you haven't got an electronics background, you may find inductance and capacitance a little daunting at first. However, they should become clearer with time and study. An understanding of alternating current is necessary and

---

Inductance, Capacitance and AC Theory Sample Questions

1) A 28v DC supply may be obtained from a 115v AC supply by using what?
2) In an AC circuit containing only capacitance, will current lead or lag the voltage?
3) On what factors is the frequency of a DC generator dependent?
4) In a reactive circuit, what is the relationship between current and voltage?
5) Why should AC generators operating in parallel have the same voltage and frequency?
6) If two AC generators are operating in parallel, in what units is the power measured?
7) In an induction motor, as slip increases, does torque increase or decrease?

TIP
You will learn that the symbol for capacitance is 'C', for current is 'I', for voltage is 'V' and for inductance is 'L'. The word 'CIVIL' has a significant pattern in its letters and will prove a useful memory jogger in an exam. In a capacitive circuit, 'I' leads 'V' (C I V); 'V' leads 'I' in an inductive circuit (V I L).

should build gradually throughout your study of electrics. One concept that is vital is the relationship between voltage and current in capacitive and inductive circuits – it is rare for a JAA exam to go by without a question on this.

Three-Phase Electrics
The subject of three-phase electrics forms a prominent part of the syllabus; the system is widely used, so it must be understood. You need to know why three-phase electrics is used. The syllabus covers the different types of AC generator and motor. Many types of generator (such as salient-pole, brushless and constant-speed) will be studied, and a basic knowledge of their differences and characteristics is required. This also applies to AC motors (induction, two-phase induction, split-phase, single-phase commutator and synchronous). In three-phase electrics, regulation and protection systems, fault protection systems, load sharing, auxiliary power units (APU) and ram-air turbine (RAT) systems are all featured, and a basic knowledge of them is necessary.

Three-Phase Electrics Sample Questions

1) One of the phases of a star-wound, three-phase system is accidentally earthed. How many of its phases will be earthed?
2) In a typical aircraft AC system, how many volts is the phase voltage?
3) In a three-phase, star-connected AC generator, by how many degrees are the phases out of phase?
4) What is the purpose of a constant-speed drive unit?

Semiconductors
The Electrics syllabus also covers electrical consumers, such as lighting, de-icing, engine starting and avionics equipment. A basic knowledge of these is required, such as whether they are resistive and how much power they consume. Semiconductors are included too, and an understanding of their structure and use is required. This leads on to a study of diodes and transistors.

Semiconductors Sample Questions

1) Does a semiconductor have a high or low resistance to current flow?
2) What are the base materials used in the manufacture of semiconductors?

Logic Circuits and Computing
Lastly in Electrics are logic circuits and computers. Although you will need to study a number of systems, binary is normally the subject of any questions asked in exams.

Logic circuits are also shown in the exam, and practice in decoding circuits is probably the best way to learn them. It is important to have a basic knowledge of computers as well, such as the various components and the difference between hardware and software.

> **TIP**
> Calculators are available that have a binary button. They are allowed in the JAA exam, making binary conversions very quick and easy.

Logic Circuits and Computing Sample Questions

1) What is the function of a NOT logic gate within a circuit?
2) In computer technology, what may be described as an output peripheral?
3) In computer technology, what may be described as an input peripheral?
4) In computer technology, what may be described as a storage peripheral?
5) What is the binary equivalent of the number 8?

Engines

Engines fall into two categories: gas turbine and piston. As an airline pilot, you could fly both. I found engines an enjoyable subject, as it was very interesting, and I could easily relate to it from experiences with my car and previous flying lessons. Engines are broken down into the following subject areas.

- Basic Laws
- Piston-Engine Construction and Systems
- Piston-Engine Performance and Faults
- Power Augmentation Devices
- Gas-Turbine Engine Construction and Systems
- Variable-Pitch Propellers

Basic Laws

As with many subjects, it is important to understand some of the basic laws of the science. To understand engines, you should also have an appreciation of the general gas laws – such as Boyle's and Charles' – the laws of pressure and the way heat is transferred (conduction, convection and radiation). Newton's laws are relevant to the study of engines too, as they can be used in thrust calculations for propellers and gas turbines.

Basic Laws Sample Questions

1) Which law considers the tendency of an object to remain at rest or in uniform motion?
2) Which process can be used to describe the transfer of heat from the cylinder fins of the engine to the cooling air?

Piston-Engine Construction and Systems

A knowledge of piston-engine construction is essential for the JAA exams and because you will be using piston engines throughout your initial flying training, spending many hours behind one on long solo flights! The

---

TIP

Revise your Radio Navigation notes for AGK too. There are often a few simple radio navigation questions, such as: What frequency does MLS use? What is the wavelength of a VOR?

TIPS

$$\text{Indicated horsepower} = \frac{\text{Mean Pressure} \times \text{Length of Stroke} \times \text{Piston Area} \times \text{RPM}/2 \times \text{No. of Cylinders}}{60\sec \times 550}$$

This can be remembered as: $\dfrac{\text{P L A N K (Pressure} \times \text{Length} \times \text{Area} \times \text{RPM (N)} \times \text{Cylinders [constant, K])}}{60 \times 550}$

The colours of the different types of fuel need to be known, and they can be remembered by writing them down in number order, starting with the highest, then writing their colours in alphabetical order.

Avgas 115   – Blue
Avgas 100 (HL) – Green
Avgas 100 (LL) – Lighter Blue
Avgas 80   – Red

The carburettor has many different components, which are summarized by the acronym MISHAP. This may help you to remember how the carburettor works.

M – Main metering (main jet/diffuser)
I – Idle jet
S – Stopping (slow run cut-out)
H – Height (mixture control)
A – Acceleration (accelerator pump for when throttle is opened quickly)
P – Power enrichment (economizers for leaning the mixture at low power)

You could be asked in an exam the meaning of different colours of smoke coming from an engine. This can be remembered quite simply by listing the causes and effects in alphabetical order.

Burning too much Fuel = Black smoke   (F = Bla)
Burning too much Oil = Blue smoke   (O = Blu)
Water vapour   = White Smoke   (W = W)

starting point in learning about the piston engine will be the essentials, such as the cylinders and crankshaft. These lead on to the Otto Cycle, which is the cycle of processes within the engine that make it produce power. The various engine systems, such as the carburettor, lubrication and ignition, are also vital for the exam. They can be studied individually, then linked in with the rest of the engine. All these systems are quite detailed, and it would not be appropriate to cover everything in this text. However, helpful tips and anything that is particularly important to highlight are given.

Piston-Engine Construction and Systems Sample Questions

1) What typical fuel/air ratio would be used for engine take-off power?
2) What happens to the compression ratio of a piston engine as the fuel's octane rating is increased?
3) During climb with constant manifold air pressure (MAP) and RPM indication, and constant mixture setting, what happens to the power output of a piston engine?
4) What is the term for the part of an engine that transforms reciprocating movement into rotary motion?
5) How is the brake horsepower (BHP) of a piston engine measured?
6) What is the formula for the power output of a piston engine?
7) What kind of fuel/air mixture could cause engine overheating?
8) What is compression ratio?
9) What kind of oil might be used for 'running in' a new piston engine?
10) In the correct order, what are the four stages of the Otto Cycle?

Piston-Engine Performance and Faults

Piston engines do suffer from performance problems and faults. I believe it is essential to know about these in depth, as you will be flying a piston engine for the first part of your training, and knowledge of the engine could save your life. The commonest problem with a piston engine that employs a carburettor is carburettor icing. An understanding of this is valuable, as it is also covered in the Meteorology syllabus, and you may encounter it from time to time in your flying. The exam is most likely to test that you understand carburettor icing can occur in temperatures up to 30°C.

Piston-Engine Performance and Faults Sample Questions

1) How may high exhaust gas temperatures be caused?
2) If oil pressure does not rise within thirty seconds of engine start, what would your action be?
3) What occurs if an ignition switch becomes shorted to earth at one magneto?
4) What are the symptoms of carburettor icing?
5) In which section of the carburettor is icing most likely to occur?

Engine performance will drop off as altitude increases due to changing air density; this may crop up in an exam. The ignition system is prone to problems too, such as a broken ignition-switch wire, a faulty capacitor or a fouled spark plug. You should also understand what kind of problems may cause low oil pressure or high oil temperature.

Power Augmentation Devices
Piston-engine aircraft may be fitted with power augmentation devices to increase power for take-off and climb, or to maintain engine power as altitude increases by artificially increasing manifold pressure. There are two types of device: the turbocharger and supercharger. It took me some time to gain a good understanding of these components. It is essential, however, to have a basic understanding of how the systems work, that they are driven by exhaust gases and what happens to the air pressure throughout the system. You should know about the various controllers used in dual and triple superchargers (differential pressure, density, absolute, rate and pressure ratio) and their purpose.

Power augmentation devices also suffer from problems, such as turbo lag, hunting the manifold air pressure (bootstrapping) and seized wastegates. These problems are very popular subjects for exam questions.

Power Augmentation Devices Sample Questions

1) What is a turbocharger system driven by?
2) In a piston engine, what is used to monitor turbocharger boost pressure?
3) What kind of compressor is normally used as a supercharger?
4) What would be the consequence of a seized wastegate during a descent with a fully open throttle?
5) What is the definition of full-throttle height?
6) To prevent over-boosting of a turbocharged engine during a power increase, what controller might be fitted to the engine?
7) What might happen if the wastegate actuator of a turbocharged engine loses oil pressure while the aircraft is at the critical altitude?

Gas-Turbine Engine Construction and Systems
There are many types of gas-turbine engine, so it is a big subject to study. At a basic level, however, gas-turbine engines are much simpler than piston engines, so don't be too daunted by them. The principle behind the gas-turbine engine is the Brayton Cycle (as pressure increases, volume decreases). An appreciation of this is essential to understanding the engine. A basic knowledge of the following types of gas-turbine engine should be sufficient:

• Single-entry, two-stage, centrifugal turbo propeller
• Double-entry, single-stage, centrifugal turbo jet
• Single-spool axial-flow turbo jet
• Twin-spool, by-pass turbo jet

There are many variants of jet engine to consider.

- Triple-spool, front-fan turbo jet
- Twin-spool, axial-flow turbo propeller
- Twin-spool, turbo shaft

I found it important to understand the functions of divergent and convergent ducts, and how they affect the pressure, temperature and velocity of air. The engines are made up of various different aerofoils, and you could be asked about their shapes or function in various parts of the engine. Some knowledge from the POF syllabus, including supersonic airflow, is useful here. One problem with gas-turbine engines that is often asked about is the ability of these aerofoils to stall or surge. An appreciation of the causes and indications of these problems, and which type of engine is more susceptible to them, is valuable.

The combustion chambers in a gas-turbine engine can vary widely, so you will need to know the different types and their characteristics. There are a lot of numbers to remember as well, such as the approximate temperature of the air at various parts of the chamber, and the percentages of air that actually travel through each part of the chamber. Nozzles are used to deliver fuel into the combustion chamber; again, you must be aware of a variety of types. The exhaust unit, the fuel system and engine starting will also be studied. It is important to understand the engine starting sequence (Rotation, Ignition, Fuel – RIF) and you will need to know about starting problems, such as hot, hung and cold starts.

Variable-Pitch Propellers
The variable-pitch propeller is an important part of an engine, and I found the subject quite complex. If you study it alongside POF, however, you will find that they coincide quite nicely, as there is a section on propellers in the latter's syllabus. You will need to understand the principle of operation of a constant-speed unit and what the various components do. You should know how the system corrects a propeller over-speed or under-speed, and how the propeller is feathered and unfeathered. There are two different power-lever modes, alpha and beta; you should be familiar with these and when each of them is used. Propeller synchronization and negative torque sensing are also studied in this section.

Gas-Turbine Engine Construction and Systems Sample Questions

1) What does the diffuser in a gas-turbine engine do?
2) What would be a typical axial-flow compressor outlet temperature?
3) Choose the correct answers to the following question: When would the use of igniters be necessary on a turbo jet?
   a) Throughout the operating range of the engine
   b) For accelerations
   c) For ground starts
   d) For in-flight relights
   e) During turbulence in flight
   f) Under heavy precipitation or in icing conditions
4) What is the most efficient turbine blade design for a fan-type engine?
5) Give a typical self-sustaining speed for a twin-spool turbine engine?
6) What type of oil might be used in a gas-turbine engine?
7) Why is the flow duct tapered in an axial-flow compressor?
8) What happens to pressure, velocity and temperature as gases pass through a convergent duct?
9) What is the purpose of shrouding stator blade tips?
10) What would be the ideal pressure rise across a centrifugal compressor?
11) Where does air have the highest velocity in a gas-turbine engine?

Variable-Pitch Propellers Sample Questions

1) What is the main advantage of a constant-speed propeller over a fixed-pitch propeller?
2) Using a constant-speed propeller, what combination of manifold air pressure and RPM values can lead to excessive pressure in the cylinders?
3) As true airspeed increases, what happens to the pitch angle of a constant-speed propeller?
4) Where is the pitch angle of a propeller measured?
5) What will happen to the pitch angle of a constant-speed propeller if the manifold air pressure is increased?
6) In which stages of a flight would a pilot normally use the auto-feather system?
7) During flight, the pitch angle of a propeller is 90°. What is the term for this?
8) Generally, in a twin-engine piston aircraft with a constant-speed propeller, what does the oil pressure in the constant-speed system do to the blade angle?
9) Which way do the governor flyweights move when the propeller over-speeds?
10) In respect of a constant-speed unit, to what does the term 'on-speed' refer?

TIP

Aerodynamic and centrifugal turning moments (ATM and CTM) tend to twist a propeller toward coarse and fine pitch respectively. A good way I found of remembering this was that ATM also means cash dispenser, which increases the money in your pocket. Therefore:
ATM = INCREASE in blade angle
CTM = DECREASE in blade angle

METEOROLOGY

The subject of meteorology is very wide ranging, encompassing many aspects that need to be studied. For ease of explanation, however, I will group them into more general areas and give sample questions:

- The Atmosphere and its Characteristics
- Altimetry
- Weather
- Wind
- Air Masses
- Practical Meteorology
- Climatology

The Atmosphere and its Characteristics

This subject covers the International Standard Atmosphere (ISA), temperature, density, pressure and humidity. Initially, you will learn about the structure of the atmosphere and how the temperature varies in each layer. It is essential to have an understanding of the ISA, as it occurs throughout all the subjects studied, and the knowledge will be required in most aviation related careers.

You will look at heat and temperature, exactly how the latter is measured, what affects the temperature of the Earth and the different ways in which the Earth is heated (you will need to understand the terms 'convection', 'conduction' and 'radiation'). Pressure and density must be understood as well. How they are measured, the different types of pressure system, and the factors affecting pressure and density are all covered.

Humidity is an important factor in meteorology, and you will need to know exactly what humidity is and what affects it. This requires an understanding of other terms, such as 'dew point', 'humidity mixing ratio', 'saturation vapor pressure' and 'relative humidity'. You will need to be aware

---

The Atmosphere and its Characteristics Sample Questions

1) What is the term for an increase in temperature with altitude?
2) At what height is density constant at all latitudes?
3) What is the height of the tropopause at 50°N?
4) In an ISA, at what height is the 300mb level?
5) In which layer is most of the atmospheric humidity concentrated?
6) When a given mass of air descends, what effect will this have on its relative humidity?
7) Of conduction, convection and solar radiation, which two contribute most to atmospheric warming?
8) Under what condition does pressure altitude have the same value as density altitude?

---

of how humidity is measured and the factors that affect it. A radiosonde balloon can measure meteorological values at high altitudes, and this often appears in the exam – it is worth remembering that the balloon measures pressure, temperature and humidity.

Altimetry

Understanding altimetry can be tricky, and you need lots of practice to be able to work quickly. Altimeters work on air pressure, and altimetry is used for many tasks related to this, such as calculating an aircraft's clearance from the ground when flying from one place to another where the air pressure at the destination differs from that at the departure airfield. Altimetry also crops up in the General Navigation and Instruments syllabuses, so it is vital to have a good understanding of the subject. It may seem quite complicated at first, but the best way I found of working accurately and quickly was to draw quick sketches of the scenarios given. The Q codes, such as QNH, QFE and QFF, together with the ISA values should all be fully understood before attempting any problems. The questions you are likely to be asked will only be based on simple numeracy, but beware that with multiple-choice answers, if you apply a rule the wrong way around, the wrong answer will most likely be one of the choices given.

Altimetry Sample Questions

1) QNH in Granada (1,842ft above mean sea level) is 1012hPa. What is the QFE?
2) An aerodrome at sea level has a QNH of 1014. Is the QFF higher, lower, equal or can you not tell from the information given?
3) How is QFE determined from QNH?
4) An airfield is 600ft above mean sea level with a QNH of 998mb. An aircraft lands there with the standard pressure setting selected; what will its altimeter read on landing?
5) What does a barograph record?
6) When can QNH, QFE and QFF all be equal?
7) In Geneva, the local QNH is 994hPa. The elevation of Geneva is 1,411ft. What is the QFE adjustment in Geneva?

Weather

I have called this section 'Weather' as a means of grouping such subjects as clouds, precipitation and thunderstorms. I really enjoyed learning about the different types of cloud and practising identifying them. It is easy to do when laying on the beach or just being out and about. You will need to know which clouds are stable and unstable, the altitudes that the various types can be found and the kind of weather each signifies. It is common to be given a rather strange drawing in the exam, your task being to identify the type of cloud. Perhaps the most important aspect of cloud study is knowing how they are reported, both in type and in quantity. This will crop up in your exam, and will be essential knowledge for the rest of your career as a pilot. To understand the climatology section, it is also important to have an appreciation of cloud development, such as orographic, frontal and convergence.

The different types of precipitation are coded for meteorological reports (for example, snow is 'SN'). These codes should all be known, as should the definition of each type of precipitation, how they are formed and the droplet sizes. Precipitation is also reported in intensity and duration with precise definitions; these must be memorized for the exam.

Thunderstorms are very important in aviation, as they are hazardous. Different types of thunderstorm are classified according to their trigger action – frontal, air mass and orographic – and the exam requires a knowledge and understanding of them all. You should know all the conditions that are required to create a thunderstorm, together with its life cycle, which consists of:

1. Development stage
2. Mature stage (including microburst)
3. Dissipating stage

You must know how long each of these stages lasts and the conditions that are experienced during them. The hazards of thunderstorms are the most interesting to pilots, among them turbulence, hail, icing, static electricity, pressure variations, wind shear, microburst, tornadoes and water ingestion. An understanding of these dangers, particularly icing, is vital. You should know

---

Weather Sample Questions

1) What types of cloud are classified as medium cloud?
2) In unstable air, how is surface visibility most likely to be reduced?
3) What trigger action is likely to cause local, isolated thunderstorms?
4) Which cloud type stretches across all three cloud levels?
5) Give the colours used on AWR from least to worst intensity.
6) +TSRA come from what sort of cloud?
7) Which cloud type can project into the stratosphere?
8) At what levels can hail be anticipated in association with cumulo-nimbus cloud in temperate latitudes?
9) In which stage of a thunderstorm are only up-draughts present?
10) What type of cloud may produce freezing drizzle?
11) What type of cloud is least likely to cause icing?
12) Define sublimation.
13) What type of icing requires immediate diversion?
14) What is the most severe form of icing?

TIPS

The geostrophic force results in the air following a curved path due to the differing rotational speeds of the Earth. Just remember that the path:

- Turns to right – Northern Hemisphere
- Turns to left – Southern Hemisphere.
- Is straight at the equator and curved the most at the poles.

The direction of the geostrophic wind can easily be determined using Buys Ballots Law: put your back to the wind; the lower pressure will be on your left. (For thermal wind, the lowest temperature is on your left.)

Remember, however that the opposite applies in the Southern Hemisphere.

There is also a gradient wind, which results from adding centrifugal force.

At a given latitude with the same pressure gradient force, the gradient wind speed is higher around a high [pressure] and lower around a low.

A high-pressure system is also known as an anti-cyclone; a low-pressure system as a cyclone. To remember the direction of the wind around either type of system, note that for the Southern Hemisphere:

- If it is an ANTI-cyclone, the wind blows ANTI-clockwise around it.
- If it is a cyclone, it blows clockwise.

---

the cause of icing, the temperature ranges of super-cooled water droplets and all the different types of icing, both in the air and on the ground. To describe the amounts of icing encountered, there is an 'airframe icing intensity criteria', which should be learned. It will also be useful for your career to be aware of the factors that affect ice accumulation, such as speed, aerodynamics and orographic intensification. Engine icing is part of the syllabus as well, but you should be proficient in this aspect from the Engines syllabus.

In the Instruments syllabus, you will study the Airborne Weather Radar (AWR); this also occurs in the Meteorology syllabus, as it helps pilots to avoid thunderstorms. You will learn the principle of operation and how to use the system. Depending on altitude, AWR echoes should be avoided by specific distances; these figures are important and should be committed to memory.

Wind

Although wind may appear to be a tricky area of meteorology, it can be thought of in quite simple ways: there are low-level winds, upper winds and local winds. You need to know the instrument used to measure wind and under what conditions it should be placed. 'Gust', 'lull', 'squall', 'gale' and 'tropical storm' are all terms with which you will become familiar, and for each you will need to know the related wind speed range. Many low-level winds can be difficult to understand, such as the geostrophic wind, which comprises a geostrophic force and a pressure gradient force.

> **TIP**
> To calculate the upper wind, draw a rough vector diagram by eye; the resultant vector will give you the upper wind. If the direction of the thermal wind component is not given, use Buys Ballots Law.

Wind Sample Questions

1) What is the direction of airflow in a land breeze?
2) What is the typical width, length and height of a jet stream?
3) When will ATC report wind as gusting?
4) Which force prevents wind from flowing directly from high to low pressure?
5) Describe a katabatic wind.
6) Planning a flight at Flight Level 290, which upper wind and temperature chart are you most likely to use for planning?
7) Where is an anemometer placed?
8) What types of jet stream can be observed all year round?
9) If the wind at 5000ft is 300°/20kt and the thermal wind component is 40kt, what is the upper wind in the Northern Hemisphere, with cold air to the north?
10) Define wind shear.

Surface wind is caused by all of the forces plus the surface friction force. The friction will vary, however, especially between land and sea. This will affect the amount by which the wind changes direction and speed, and you should know the approximate figures for the difference between land and sea.

High and low pressures also cause convergence and divergence, which create weather, so you should be familiar with these, as well as the diurnal variation of wind speed and direction.

Upper winds are created by pressure differential, and you will learn how to interpret weather charts. To calculate an upper wind, you need to know the thermal wind component and the geostrophic wind. You also should be aware of the global thermal winds.

Jet streams are important to aviation, so you should study their size, strength, location, turbulence and wind directions. They also occur around fronts, and you will need to know their characteristics and where they are to be found. It is important to understand the location and hazards of clear-air turbulence as well.

Local winds must be considered when planning a flight that lands at a coastal airfield – you may experience winds that are very different from the forecast winds due to the unequal heating of the land and the sea. An understanding of sea breezes is essential: when they are likely to be present and how land breezes differ. Katabatic and anabatic winds also occur due to temperature changes; you need to know how these come about and where they are most common.

> **TIP**
> Remember that cold air is denser than warm air, so will always push underneath
> the latter when they meet. Therefore:
>
> - A warm front occurs when the warm air overrides the cold air.
> - A cold front occurs when the cold air undercuts the warm air.
> - A quasi-stationary front occurs when the two air masses have very little
>   interaction.

The Föhn wind, found around mountain ranges, is also a frequent subject
of questions. You should be able to explain how and when it occurs, in terms
of stability and lapse rates.

In addition, you need to know about valley winds and headland winds,
both of which are created by a venturi effect.

Air Masses

Large volumes of air, stretching thousands of miles, are known as air masses.
Each has a source region – Tropical, Polar or Arctic – and a humidity type,
either continental or maritime. At this point of the course, you should know
the type of weather an air mass may bring. For example, a cold air mass flowing over a cold surface is likely to produce stable weather conditions.

Fronts come about when two air masses come together. There are warm,
cold and quasi-stationary fronts.

You will need to be able to calculate the speed of a front, which is often
asked in the exam. A good way to do this is to determine the geostrophic
wind speed by measuring the distance between the isobars at the front. For
a warm front, the speed is two-thirds that of the geostrophic wind.

Polar front depressions and occlusions play a large part in the UK's
weather, so you will need to know all about them – how they are formed,
where they exist, their associated weather and clouds, the winds and temperatures, and the period of their life cycle. A polar front depression is split into
a warm sector and a cold sector, and you should understand the differences
between the two. Occlusions are split into three different air masses, and you
should be aware of the hazards of the various combinations.

As well as fronts, there are depressions (cyclones) and anti-cyclones. You will
need to know about the various types of depression. These comprise
secondary depressions, polar lows, thermal depressions, orographic depressions,
continental lows, the inter-tropical convergence zone (ITCZ, which is extremely
important for the Climatology section), tropical revolving storms, tornadoes,
cold pools and troughs of low pressure. You should be able to explain all of these
phenomena and have an idea of where they are most commonly formed.

The various types of anti-cyclone must be understood – permanent
warm, temporary warm, permanent cold, temporary cold, blocking, ridges,
and cols.

Air Masses Sample Questions

1) Why do tropical revolving storms tend not to occur in the south-east Pacific or the south Atlantic?
2) What is the diameter of a typical tornado?
3) What type of low is usually associated with frontal activity?
4) What is the source region of tropical maritime affecting the UK?
5) What is the movement of air aloft, relating to a ridge?
6) What conditions of a cold pool may be observed from the ground?
7) What is the typical weather found within a col in the summer?
8) Where is the coldest air to be found in an occlusion with cold-front characteristics?
9) What weather conditions may occur when an Arctic maritime air mass reaches the UK coast?
10) When do cold occlusions occur most frequently in Europe?
11) What type of low-pressure area is associated with a surface front?

TIPS

At the start of your course, try to collect the old METARS and TAFS from your operations department so that you have something to practise decoding.

CAVOK is a common term, but it is often misinterpreted as meaning the weather is okay. Make sure you know the true definition for the exam.

Practical Meteorology

The subject of practical meteorology concerns such activities as looking at charts for yourself, decoding them, and taking a decision on the current weather or making a forecast. If you study this section of meteorology along-side your flying, you can integrate it with your pre-flight planning. There is no easy way to learn all the different codes and numbers – I found that practice was the best for me.

You will need to know what meteorological documents are available, and understand when and why to use them. Aircraft reports are among the best source of meteorological information, and as you will be flying, you need to understand how and when to make them. Not all airports have the same weather reporting facilities, so you must be aware of what types are available and roughly how they work, such as wind shear reporting and runway visual range (RVR).

In the exam, you may be given synoptic charts to decode, so knowing the symbols employed is important; practice in using the geostrophic wind scale to measure the speed of fronts is advisable. 'Station circles' are found on synoptic charts, but they are not covered in the JAA meteorology syllabus. You will be given Metform 214 and 215 in the exam, so you should know how to interpret these. You should expect any question, but for Metform 214,

> **TIPS**
> Upper air charts can look very confusing at first. The faint black lines that separate the different areas are difficult to read. I found the charts easier to interpret if I used a coloured pen to highlight the different zones.
>
> For all of the charts mentioned, make sure you read all of the notes. Quite often, you will be asked a question that seems very difficult, but the answer will be printed in plain English at the side of the chart!

Practical Meteorology Sample Questions

(Most questions in this section will involve interpreting charts, so the best way of preparing is to get hold of some and practise decoding them.)

1) In which weather report would you expect to find information about icing conditions on the runway?
2) A VOLMET broadcast is a plain-language transmission of which meteorological report?
3) Interpret the following SIGMET:
   MOD TO SEV CAT FCST SOUTH OF ALPS BTN FL 290 AND FL 360/INTSF
4) What is the meaning of the following symbol?

5) In what units are upper-level winds forecast?
6) Where would a pilot find information about the presence of a jet stream?

---

it is likely that you will be asked the temperature and wind velocity for a given position, using the data given. For Metform 215, you may be asked to decode parts of the forecast, or describe the expected weather at a given position.

Finally, you need a knowledge of the many symbols and abbreviations found on upper air charts.

Climatology

All of your new-found meteorological knowledge comes together in climatology. I found this a very enjoyable part of the syllabus. It is quite systematic, but the basics are a little complicated to explain. The globe is split into various climatic zones due to the movement of air in cells, known as Polar, Ferrel and Hadley. You need to know why the cells come about and how they make up the climatic zones, what latitudes these zones cover and what weather can be expected in them.

The world's temperature and pressure distributions have a well-defined pattern for both summer and winter, and you should have knowledge of these for the exam.

> **TIP**
> Knowing the position of the ITCZ is vital to an understanding of global climatology. The way I learned it was to prepare a very rough sketch map of the world, make a lot of copies and keep practising drawing in the ITCZ line for both January and July. Do this many times so that when you take the exam, the first thing you do is sketch a map (look through the exam appendices, though, as you may have been given one) and draw on the lines without even thinking.

The prevailing winds are also important in global climatology. You will need to know the pattern of air flow and the position of the inter-tropical convergence zone (ITCZ), where these winds barely exist. Surface winds follow the local surface pressure patterns and topographical features, so you must have an appreciation of where the monsoons occur and where mountain ranges exist.

Surface winds also affect oceanic currents by driving bodies of water before them. This will affect weather conditions at the coasts of continents. Where two currents with different temperatures meet, advection fog could form (this occurs in Canada). I found that once I got to grips with these logical events I began to understand global climatology.

You will need to know the locations of the upper winds and the directions in which they flow. I found a very good method was to draw a diagram (*see* illustration) and commit it to memory so that I could reproduce it in the exam if required.

You will also be expected to have a good understanding of all the different climates around the world. There are many local weather phenomena, some of which are studied in this syllabus and must be remembered. Much of the world's climate, however, can be worked out using the knowledge of meteorology that you will acquire during the course. The way I learned regional climatology was to study the different regions one by one, then draw the details on a blank map of the area.

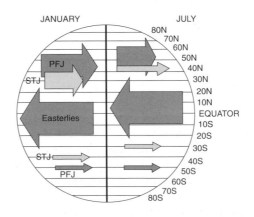

Climatology Sample Questions

1) At approximately what latitudes are the sub-tropical high-pressure belts found?
2) What weather is typical at a cold-water coast?
3) Which wind systems converge on the ITCZ when it lies at the equator?
4) When are the rains most likely in Equatorial Africa?
5) What is the main distinguishing feature of Equatorial easterly jets?
6) What is the Bora?
7) During a flight from Marseille to Dakar, where may the ITCZ be encountered?
8) What is the dominating pressure system affecting the North Atlantic in July?
9) When are thunderstorms most likely in Europe?
10) When do you get tropical revolving storms in Darwin?
11) What are tropical revolving storms off the coast of Somalia called?

The areas I studied were:

- North America and the North Atlantic
- Australia
- Asia
- Africa
- The Arctic
- Europe
- South America
- The Middle East
- The Mediterranean

For each of these areas, you need to know its climatic zone, its temperature and pressure patterns, the prevailing winds, average tropopause heights and all the local weather phenomena.

GENERAL NAVIGATION

During my study of General Navigation, I found that my fellow students either loved it or hated it. I really enjoyed the Navigation syllabus; it is one of the areas that actually aids your flying, and it is quite a practical subject. About 40 per cent of the exam involved the use of the CRP-5 navigation computer, which is an essential item for the ATPL course. There are some easier parts, such as decoding map symbols, and some harder parts, such as grid navigation. This subject also includes questions from the Instruments syllabus, about the inertial navigation system for example. I will not include these here, as they will be covered under Instruments later. The key to success in this subject is practice. The exam is tight for time, so the more you practise, especially on the CRP-5, the better your chances.

> **TIP**
> The way I remembered the difference between latitude and longitude was to call latitude, 'flatitude' (latitude is the flat – horizontal – line, not the vertical line).

General Navigation can be split into the following areas:

- The Earth
- The CRP-5
- Earth Convergence and Conversion Angle
- Scale
- Charts
- Pilot Navigation Techniques
- Point of Equal Time (PET) and Point of Safe Return (PSR)
- Grid Navigation
- Time

The Earth

To study navigation in detail, a general knowledge of the form of the Earth is required. This includes the cardinal directions, its shape and the definitions of terminology used, such as 'great circle' and 'rhumb line'. You will also need to be confident in using latitudes and longitudes.

It is very important to understand that the real North Pole is not the pole to which your compass points. The magnetic force that attracts the needle of your compass is some way away from the geographical North Pole. This gives a variation that must be applied. A compass also suffers from deviation due to other local magnetic fields, and a suitable correction must be made. For General Navigation and the other subjects, you need to be very conversant with these techniques – practice makes perfect.

A change in latitude or longitude relates to a distance in nautical miles (note that nautical miles are different from the statute miles that you would use on a road map) and, depending on the latitude, a correction factor must be applied to allow for the shape of the Earth. You need to be well-versed in this now to cope with more difficult questions later. Unfortunately, you may be asked questions in a whole range of units – nautical miles, kilometres, statute miles and feet – so you should know all of the conversion factors from memory.

Finally, for the form of the Earth, you need to know how to find the difference between two longitudes or latitudes. It sounds easy, but remember that they are not decimal numbers; they are measured in minutes and seconds. Also, be careful when subtracting from a low number. You might think that 10° minus 355° would give a difference of –345°. That would be wrong, however, since there are 360° in a circle; the answer is 15° difference. Be careful!

> **TIP**
> Try to obtain a calculator with a degrees and minutes button; it will save a lot of time in the exam.

The Earth Sample Questions

1) What is the name given to the Equatorial plane of the earth?
2) What is the maximum value of variation?
3) What is the term 'secular change' used to describe?
4) Given a compass heading of 315°, a deviation of 3°E and a variation of 15°W, what is the magnetic heading?
5) What is the shortest rhumb-line track and distance from 51°N 175°W to 51°N 175°E?
6) An aircraft at position 50°N 005°W flies north for 180nm, then east for 180nm. What is the new position of the aircraft?
7) What are parallels of latitude known as (except the Equator)?

The CRP-5

It is absolutely essential that you are quick and confident in handling the CRP-5 navigation computer. It may be needed for almost half of the exam questions, and since it is a time consuming instrument to use, you must practise to become as quick as possible. The other tip I would give is to try to do each calculation in your head as well as on the CRP-5. This will provide an approximate check that the answer you obtain from the computer is correct. There are two sides to the CRP-5: one is for conversions and the other for triangle-of-velocities calculations. You need to be fully conversant with all of the functions; the instruction book that comes with the instrument is very useful for teaching yourself. You will use the CRP-5 for working with:

- Distances
- Speeds
- Weights
- Volumes
- Specific gravity
- Temperatures
- Airspeeds
- Mach numbers
- Altitudes
- Solving vector triangles for wind speeds
- Calculating crosswind and tailwind components

Earth Convergence and Conversion Angle

The Earth convergence and conversion angles are employed in producing different types of chart, so they are studied before you start looking at the

---

CRP-5 Sample Questions

1) If the temperature is 17°C, what is this in Fahrenheit?
2) Runway 22 is in use. The wind direction is 170°M. A minimum headwind component of 10kt is required to take off and the maximum crosswind allowed is 15kt. What is the minimum wind speed required to ensure a headwind component of 10kt?
3) If the corrected outside air temperature (COAT) is –50°C and the Mach number is 0.83, what is the true airspeed (TAS)?
4) If pressure altitude is 9000ft, and COAT is –35°C, what is the true altitude?
5) What is the weight in kilograms of 165ltr of fuel at a specific gravity of 0.8?
6) An aircraft on a TMG of 310°M is maintaining a heading of 301°M, and variation is 5°W. If the TAS is 210kt and the GS 185kt, what is the wind velocity (W/V) acting on the aircraft?
7) If an aircraft climbs at a constant CAS, what happens to TAS and Mach number?

---

types of chart available. Earth convergence is the angle of inclination between the meridians – at the Equator, the lines are parallel, so there is no convergence; near the poles, however, it is at a maximum. To calculate convergence, there is a simple formula. The conversion angle must also be understood. It is the angle between the great circle and the rhumb line between any two points, and it is half the value of earth convergence. It is used to convert bearings that are great-circle directions into rhumb-line directions.

Earth Convergence and Conversion Angle Sample Questions

1) What is required to change a rhumb-line direction into a great-circle direction?
2) What is the formula for conversion angle?
3) What is the outbound direction of the great-circle track between 30°S 60°W and 30°S 20°E?
4) What is the initial great-circle track from A (30°S 175°E) to B (30°S 145°W)?
5) What is the outbound direction of the great-circle track between 60°N 165°E and 60°N 165°W?

Scale

It is important to use scales, especially on charts. Scale is a small area to be examined, but it is useful for the other subjects too. As with the CRP-5, if you are quick and accurate, you can gain easy marks in the exam. You need to know how scales can be expressed, as a fraction or ratio for example. You should also be able to convert between different units quickly and know how to calculate the scale factor.

Scale Sample Questions

1) A length of 8in represents an surface distance of 67km. What is the scale?
2) A chart has a scale of 1:3,000,000. What does 3.5in on this chart represent?
3) A chart represents 30 statute miles by 40cm. What is the chart's scale?
4) If 1.78cm represents a distance of 8.12km, what is the scale of the chart as a fraction?

Charts

I found charts to be quite challenging; it was difficult to achieve a good understanding of how the various charts work and how they are made. Different types of chart are used for different purposes. Making a chart is not easy, as it is not possible to represent the spherical shape of the Earth on flat paper with absolute accuracy. The common types of chart are:

- Mercator (normal, transverse or oblique)
- Lamberts
- Polar

You will need to have an understanding of how all three types are made, their properties, and their advantages and disadvantages. For example, some will show straight rhumb lines, while others will not; some will have a constant scale, others will not. You will also need to know the type of information they provide. The Polar chart, for example, is better for mapping areas near the poles.

During your flying and for the General Navigation exam, you must have an understanding of the topographical features shown on charts. You should know the symbols and how to read the relief. You will also need to know the value of the features in pinpointing your position or updating your ETA. This knowledge is useful for your flying training, and you may be asked a question on it in the exam. You will need to have an idea of how to make a plan for your flight that involves calculating magnetic headings, drifts and true airspeeds, all of which you will have covered in the CRP-5 section. It is unlikely that you will be required to fill in a flight plan during the exam, but

---

TIP

The Polar stereographic chart has an expanding scale as you move away from the poles. A typical exam question would ask for the value of the expansion at a given latitude. It will usually ask for the expansion at 80° or 70°. Instead of working this out each time, just remember that at 80° it is 1 per cent and 70° it is 3 per cent. You are not likely to be asked for the expansion at lower latitudes; between the two, you could try extrapolation. It will save a lot of precious time.

Charts Sample Questions

1) An aircraft departs from A at 1515 on track 090°M to fly a distance 425nm to B. Given Mach 0.8, temperature –45°C, wind velocity 060°T/20kt, mean variation 10°W, find the magnetic heading to steer and ETA at B.

2) What is the magnetic track and distance from WTD NDB (52°12′N 007°05′W) to Kerry NDB (52°12′N 009°32′W)?

3) To what does the term 'orthomorphism' refer when used to describe charts?

4) On a Normal Mercator chart, how does scale vary?

5) For what purpose is a Normal Mercator normally used?

6) The scale of a Mercator is 1:5,000,000 at 10°N. What is the scale of the chart at 35°N?

7) How do rhumb lines appear on a Transverse Mercator?

8) What is the constant of the cone for a Lamberts chart, the standard parallels of which are 13°40′N and 42°20′N?

9) A straight line drawn on a Polar stereographic chart joins X (70°N 102°W) to Y (80°N 006°E). The point of highest latitude on this line occurs at 035°W. What is the direction of the initial straight-line track measured at X?

10) What is the meaning of the following chart symbol?

$$\boxed{\textbf{\textit{17456}}}$$

---

there may be questions about them. You may be asked to determine the position of an aircraft when given a bearing and a distance from a point, or a distance from two points (this involves drawing arcs, so have a good pair of compasses handy). You may also be asked to calculate the aircraft's position at a particular time, given its current speed, position and time.

Pilot Navigation Techniques

When you are in the air and busy flying the aircraft, you will use a number of simple techniques to calculate angles, such as heading corrections and glide slopes, without the need to employ calculators or complicated sums. If you are a competent mathematician, you may find this exam frustrating. For example, you may be given a relatively complicated problem that you could solve mathematically, but you will be required to use the simplified methods to find an approximate answer. You will need to be able to use the '1 in 60' rule to calculate track error and closing angle, the height of a glide slope, rate of descent required, runway slopes, gradients and distance off track. You will also need to be confident in using nautical ground miles (NGM) and nautical air miles (NAM), as they often appear in exam questions and can be confusing.

The Point of Equal Time and Point of Safe Return

This section is not too difficult once you have practised the questions a few times. They require a lot of attention to detail and accuracy, however, as it

Pilot Navigation Techniques Sample Questions

1) At 75nm from VOR A at FL350, you start a descent to arrive over a VOR at FL100 at a groundspeed of 240kt. What rate of descent is required?
2) The distance from A to C is 120nm. B lies on the straight-line track between A and C, being 50nm from C. The TAS is 130kt, the actual time of departure from A was 1235, and the estimated time of arrival at B was 1250, whereas the actual time of arrival at B was 1253. What is the estimated time of arrival at C?
3) An ILS procedure results in the aircraft intercepting a 3° glide slope at the Outer Marker at a range of 3.5nm. Use the 1 in 60 rule to determine the approximate height at which the glide slope is intercepted.
4) An aircraft is to descend from FL180 to 3,000ft at CAS 180kt along a track of 060°T. If the time in the descent is fourteen minutes, what is the ground distance travelled?

PET/PSR Sample Questions

1) Define the Point of Safe Return.
2) What effect would there be on the PSR if in flight, the TAS was increased and the endurance unchanged?
3) Given the following information, calculate the position of the PET and ETA at the PET:

   - ATD 0415 UTC
   - Distance between airports, 830nm
   - Track 075°M
   - TAS 180kt
   - W/V 050°M/40kt

4) Calculate the position and time to the single-engine PNR, given the following information:

   - Flight fuel available (for PNR) 385ltr
   - Asymmetric TAS 110kt
   - Asymmetric fuel flow 85ltr/h
   - Normal cruise TAS 150kt
   - Normal cruise fuel flow 100ltr/h
   - Wind component outbound 40kt TAIL
   - Homebound 30kt HEAD

TIP
Beware when correcting your airspeed for wind. Unless the wind component is exactly head/tail, you cannot simply reverse the wind speed for the return leg, as you will need to balance the drift (which is covered in the CRP-5 section).

is easy to make a mistake, and these questions are normally worth a lot of marks. It is worthwhile attempting to become very competent with these subjects now, as they also form a major part of the Flight Planning exam. It is important to understand the difference between a PET and a PSR (sometimes referred to as the Point of No Return, PNR). There are simple formulas for calculating these, only one change to the formula being necessary when switching between PET and PSR. Often, you will be asked what appears to be a relatively simple PET/PSR question, but the reason such a question attracts a lot of marks is because you will be given a wind velocity that will affect your airspeed, so you need to use the CRP-5 to make the correction. Then, you may be given a single-engine airspeed and asked for an ETA back to the departure airfield. The PSR can also be calculated to give distance from departure to PNR using the fuel available and fuel flow.

Grid Navigation

I found grid navigation a difficult subject to grasp. Once I had devised a good method of using the technique, however, it did become clear. It involves laying a grid over some point of the Earth, the top of that grid becoming 'grid North'. The system allows you to select a 'grid track', which will remain constant throughout a journey, whereas a true track would change. Again, practising this technique is the key to success.

Grid Navigation Sample Questions

1) Assume a North Polar stereographic chart, the grid of which is aligned with the Greenwich meridian. An aircraft flies from the geographic North Pole for a distance of 480nm along the 120°E meridian, then follows a grid track of 146° for a distance of 300nm. What is the approximate position of the aircraft?

2) A South Polar stereographic chart is overprinted with a false grid aligned with the prime meridian. If at 85°S 125°W, the true track is 179°, what is the grid track?

3) A South Polar stereographic chart is printed with a false grid aligned with the Greenwich anti-meridian. If at 80°S 101°E, the grid track is 180°, what is the true track?

Time

This is an interesting subject that requires a lot of thought. A typical question that you can expect will ask you for the time of arrival after taking off from one time zone and flying for a long period of time to another, often crossing the international date line, so it can become confusing, particularly when deciding on the day you arrive! You will need to know a little about how the solar system operates and the Earth's position relative to the sun, together with the various terminologies for these positions and dates on which they occur. You will also need an appreciation of how the

---

Time Sample Questions

1) What is the duration of morning civil twilight at 45°N 002°W on 5 July?
2) On which date is the Earth closest to the sun?
3) On which date does the winter solstice occur?
4) An aircraft departs from Guam at 2300 Standard Time on 30 April local date. After a flight of eleven hours, fifteen minutes, it lands at Los Angeles (California). What is the Standard Time and local date of arrival (assume summer-time rules)?
5) The time in Madrid is 1345 UTC; what is the time in Helsinki UTC?
6) At 1330 UTC on 7 May, what is the Standard Time and local date in the Tonga Islands (22°S 170°W)?
7) The LMT at F (50°N 64°E) is 1430 on 26 July, what is the LMT at G (84°N 110°W)?

Earth is oriented and what causes the seasons, the long and short days. The measurement of time is important too, and you will need a good understanding of how the degrees of longitude convert into time. The different types of time, such as Local Mean Time (LMT) and Co-ordinated Universal Time (UTC), should be understood thoroughly. Exam questions often ask about sunrise, sunset, morning and evening civil twilight so you will need to know the definitions of these.

As a pilot, you will not always observe the hours of daylight from the ground, so you must be aware of how altitude affects your day. In the exam, you will be provided with an almanac containing all the times of sunrise, sunset and length of twilight at various locations around the planet. It will also include time-zone differences.

RADIO NAVIGATION

Initially, I found Radio Navigation very difficult. The principles of radio waves and wave propagation were hard to grasp. As the subject developed, however, and the actual navigation systems were studied, it became quite enjoyable and much more interesting. The exam was not too hard either, but there were a lot more questions about the Global Positioning System (GPS) than I had anticipated; this was also true of successive courses. Radio Navigation can be split into the following subject areas:

- Radio Principles and Radio Communications
- Radio Navigation Systems
- Radar and Distance Measuring Equipment
- Hyperbolic Navigation Systems
- Global Positioning System
- Area Navigation (RNAV)
- Flight Management Systems (FMS) and Electronic Displays

> **TIP**
> This useful mnemonic for the frequency spectrum should help you remember all of the frequency bands:
>
> VLF – Very
> LF   – Lovely
> MF   – Mothers
> HF   – Have
> VHF – Very
> UF   – Useful
> SHF – Sewing
> EHF – Equipment

Radio Principles and Radio Communications

Unless you have studied radio-wave principles or can remember your secondary-school physics lessons, you may find this subject quite a challenge. The radio-wave terminology must be understood, together with the vital relationship between frequency and wavelength. You will need to be able to explain the phase shift of waves, their polarization and wave modulation. ICAO has applied a coding system to waves, which relates to their modulation and the type of information transmitted. It is not absolutely vital to commit all of these codes to memory, but you need to know the most common. The frequency system must be memorized, however, as it will allow you to answer many simple exam questions.

Also, try to commit the frequency ranges, wavelengths and the use of the waves to memory. This will ensure a couple of guaranteed marks at least.

An understanding of the propagation of waves, and refraction, reflection, diffraction and attenuation will be useful as well, especially later, when looking at some of the properties of systems.

Radio communications will play an important part in your career, since you will use them to talk with ATC units and other aircraft. There are various methods of radio communication, and you need to know the properties, advantages and disadvantages of all of them. They include:

- HF communication
- VHF communication
- SELCAL (Selective Calling – allows ATC to alert a crew to an incoming radio message by means of a warning light or sounder)
- SATCOM (Satellite Communication)
- ACARS (Aircraft Communications Addressing and Reporting System – a computer link between aircraft and company operations for passing commercial and engineering messages)

Radio Navigation Systems

The radio navigation systems that are studied on this course are Ground Direction Finding (GDF), Automatic Direction Finding (ADF), VHF

Radio Principles and Radio Communications Sample Questions

1) What wavelength corresponds to a frequency of 345kHz?
2) What is the frequency range of a Super High Frequency?
3) What distance does the ionosphere lie from the earth's surface?
4) In which frequency band would you expect the shortest surface wave range?
5) To what does the ICAO designator J3E refer and how is it modulated?
6) On what frequency do SATCOM satellites receive messages, and on what frequency do they transmit them to the ground?
7) What data link system provides communications between the aircraft and the airline?

Omni-directional Radio Range (VOR), Instrument Landing System (ILS) and the Microwave Landing System (MLS). For each, you will need to know the properties, advantages, disadvantages, limitations, accuracy and how they work. For GDF, you also need to have an appreciation of the classifications of accuracy for each system and the codes used to explain the type of bearing (e.g. QTE, QDR). As a rule, ADF employs a Non-Directional Beacon (NDB) as the source of its radio waves. When you start the instrument phase of your flying training, you will use NDBs often, so gaining a good understanding of them at this stage should help you later. Since the aircraft you will fly will be fitted with ADF, you should understand how the aerial that receives the radio waves works and what it looks like. You will also need to operate the ADF control unit, so a thorough study of that will be useful.

VOR differs from ADF in that it is not affected by so many problems. Again, the principles of operation of VOR should be understood, as you will be using the system very frequently both in your instrument flying and your visual flying. You will need to know how to use a typical VOR indicator and a Radio Magnetic Indicator (RMI), which is an alternative VOR indicator. You must also know how to calculate the range of a VOR.

Probably the most important navigation aid in modern flying, the ILS is employed on most airline approaches, and throughout your training, you will conduct many ILS approaches. The ILS is based at the airport and

A typical layout of radio navigation systems. This is what you can expect to see in your training aircraft.

Radio Navigation Systems Sample Questions

1) A GDF bearing is given as 'Class Bravo'. What is the accuracy of this information?
2) What are the causes of error to VDF bearings?
3) What is the purpose of the Beat Frequency Oscillator (BFO) selector on an ADF receiver?
4) What factors are liable to affect NDB/ADF system performance and reliability?
5) In which frequency band do VOR transmitters operate?
6) An aircraft flying at FL110 wishes to obtain weather information at the destination airfield from the airfield's VOR. What is the maximum theoretical range at which it will be possible to obtain this information?
7) How many degrees of coverage does an ILS glide path provide in azimuth?
8) Where in relation to the runway is an ILS localizer transmitting aerial normally situated?
9) What are the major ground-based components of the MLS system?
10) The azimuth transmitter of the MLS provides a fan-shaped approach zone; how many degrees either side of the runway centreline does this normally cover?

requires a fairly complex arrangement of equipment, with which you should be familiar. You will need to know how to use and read the airborne equipment, and understand all of the limitations of the system. An ILS can be split into three categories, depending on the certification of the equipment; each category allows you to use the ILS down to different minima, all of which you should have memorized. The MLS is a development of the ILS, providing multiple approach paths, lots of channels, a curved approach path and automatic data transfer. It is rarely used in the real world, but it is in the JAR syllabus, so you do need an understanding of its operation.

Radar and Distance Measuring Equipment

You will need to know the principles of radar operation. You must understand the meaning of all the radar terminology, the basic radar system and how to calculate its range. Two types of radar – primary and secondary – are covered in this syllabus, so you will learn about both systems. The factors affecting the use, limitations and accuracy of radar systems will also be studied. A common exam question will ask for the typical specifications of a certain type of radar system (e.g. precision approach or surface movement), such as its range, frequency or even beam width, so it is well worth committing these to memory. After learning the principles, you will study the following radar systems:

- Secondary Surveillance Radar
- Distance Measuring Equipment (DME)
- Airborne Weather Radar (also studied in Meteorology)
- Doppler Radar

Radar and Distance Measuring Equipment Sample Questions

1) What is the maximum range of radar that has a pulse recurrence interval of 1500μsec?
2) To double the range of a radar transmitter, by how much must its power be increased?
3) How many possibilities are there for mode A replies?
4) At what deviation from an assigned altitude received by mode C replies will an air traffic controller assume that an aircraft has changed its level?
5) To indicate a radio failure, what code should a pilot select on his transponder?
6) On a DME indicator, what do display counters that are rotating throughout their range indicate?
7) To find out if a cloud return on an AWR is at, or above, the height of the aircraft, to how many degrees should the tilt control be set?
8) What are the main factors that determine whether or not a cloud can be detected by AWR?
9) An aircraft moving toward a transmitter emitting a frequency of 9gHz detects a Doppler shift of 5kHz. What is the speed of the aircraft?

Hyperbolic Navigation Systems

Although quite old and rarely used, hyperbolic navigation systems do form part of the JAR syllabus. Before looking into the navigation systems themselves, you will need an understanding of the hyperbolic principle. This seems quite complex at first, but it will become much clearer with some simple study. Once the principles have been explained, you will go on to learn about LORAN C, which stands for 'long-range aid to navigation'. It is a fairly complicated system, but all you really need to know is the principle of its operation, together with its accuracy, errors and coverage.

Hyperbolic Navigation Sample Questions

1) What is the principle of operation of LORAN C?
2) In what frequency band does LORAN C operate?
3) What is the maximum range of LORAN C when using surface waves?

Global Positioning System

GPS is a modern and accurate form of navigation that employs satellite ranging. I found that there were lots of questions on the principles of GPS in the exam, so a thorough knowledge of how it works is advisable. You will need to know how many satellites there are and how many are required to produce a position fix. Also, you must have an appreciation of the GPS frequencies and the contents of the GPS navigation message, together with its accuracy and errors, and the developments that have been introduced to overcome them. You will find that the GPS has three segments, comprising

---

GPS Sample Questions

1) In the GPS system, how is receiver clock error overcome?
2) 'Selective availability' degrades the accuracy of a GPS system; what method is used to achieve this?
3) In relation to GPS, the term 'inclination' is the angle between which two planes?
4) What is the maximum amount of time taken to receive the almanac data from all the GPS satellites?
5) What are the errors that affect the accuracy of GPS?
6) How many satellites need to be in view to obtain a three-dimensional fix without barometric aiding?

---

the satellites themselves, the control centre in the USA and the user (your GPS unit). You must be well-versed on these segments for the exam. GLONASS is a similar system, having been developed by the USSR; you should know a little about this as well. As you will be using GPS, you may be examined on the types of GPS receiver and its facilities.

Area Navigation

RNAV allows an aircraft to track on any flight path it chooses, provided it is in range of required navigation aids. This helps to reduce flight time, fuel consumption and congestion over beacons. You may well use RNAV in your instrument flying training, and I am sure that you will find it very useful. You should be aware of the different types of RNAV system, their outputs, problems and the basic principle behind their operation.

Area Navigation Sample Questions

1) Give an air data input for an RNAV system.
2) Which type of beacon will provide the most accurate RNAV fix?
3) What track-keeping accuracy (in nm) is required of a Precision RNAV system?
4) What is the accuracy of Basic RNAV (in nm)?
5) On a five-dot indicator using RNAV, in the en-route mode, how many miles does one dot represent?

Flight Management Systems and Electronic Displays

The Instruments syllabus covers most aspects of the flight management system and electronic displays, but you can expect some questions in the Radio Navigation exam. It is unlikely that your training aircraft will have an FMS or many electronic displays, but as an airline pilot, you will be using them on every flight. Most exam questions about FMS and electronic displays will include a picture of an electronic display, and you will be asked to describe what the display is showing. For the FMS, you will need to know

---

Flight Management Systems and Electronic Displays Sample Questions

1) In which modes of an EFIS screen are weather returns not shown?
2) On an electronic display, what is represented by the colour green?
3) On a Boeing 737-400, what colour is used to display the selected heading on the EHSI?
4) What colour is recommended in JAR-25 for the active route?
5) In the 'NAV' and 'EXPANDED NAV' modes, one dot on the EHSI represents how many nautical miles?
6) When is the FMS position likely to be least accurate?
7) Which component of the Boeing 737-400 electronic flight instrument system generates the visual displays on the EADI and EHSI?

---

what inputs it requires and the outputs it can give. You will also need to be aware of the sub-systems it utilizes.

Electronic displays usually come in the following forms:

- Electronic Flight Instrument System (EFIS)
- Engine Indication and Crew Alerting System (EICAS)
- Electronic Attitude Director Indicator (EADI)
- Electronic Horizontal Situation Indicator (EHSI)

You will need to know the components of all these displays, together with their inputs and outputs, their functions, and their advantages and disadvantages. The displays are usually coloured, the colours being standardized for specific meanings; you need to know these meanings. The EHSI can be set into different output modes, depending on your requirements. For example, it can be used in 'NAV', 'VOR' or 'ILS' mode, and for each, it can be set to 'full' or 'expanded' view. The EHSI employs a lot of symbols, which you must know, as you could be asked to decode some of them.

The control display unit (CDU) must also be studied; it is the interface between the pilot and the FMS. A rough understanding of how to use and program an FMS would be advantageous, although the exam questions normally ask for the order in which each page is displayed or the function of each button on the unit.

MASS AND BALANCE

I very much enjoyed the Mass and Balance syllabus. I found it rewarding after doing pages of simple sums to come up with the correct answer.

Along with the two communications subjects, Mass and Balance has a very special place in the course. As it is such a small subject to study and is so systematic, it is quite possible to achieve 100 per cent in the exam. If you can do this in the two small communications subjects as well, you will drastically improve your average across all of the ATPL exams. This could make or break your career, as some airlines look at your overall average and will only consider you if you achieve a set value (commonly 85 per cent).

For the Mass and Balance exam, you will be issued with a supplementary manual supplied by the CAA. This manual is absolutely vital to your success, and you should know it inside out. This does not mean memorizing it, as you may use it in the exam, but you should know where to find information and exactly what it contains. Some questions are as simple as looking up a definition in the manual.

At the end of this section is a list of five formulas; if you can remember them, the subject becomes quite simple. Beware of trick questions, however – it is easy to make a mistake when pressed for time in the exam. Practice is the key to success; you will become quicker, allowing more time to absorb the detail of each question and giving you a better chance of getting 100 per cent.

Mass and Balance can be broken down into the following subject areas:

- Aerodynamics and Stability
- Basic Empty Mass (BEM) and Centre of Gravity (cg)
- Specific Gravity (SG)
- Loading and Limitations
- Cargo
- JAR-OPS

Aerodynamics and Stability

A good understanding of the basic lift equation and aerodynamics from the POF syllabus will give you a sound foundation for this subject. You will need to know what effects an increase or decrease in weight will have on the aircraft's operating characteristics. The POF syllabus will also cover stability, and you will need to know this for the Mass and Balance exam, which will be concerned with such aspects as the various effects on the aircraft and its characteristics of a change in position of the centre of gravity or centre of pressure. The three types of stability (positive, neutral and negative) should also be understood.

Aerodynamics and Stability Sample Questions

1) The weight of an aircraft in level and non-accelerated flight is said to act through what point?
2) How many points of support are required to measure the mass and centre of gravity of an aircraft?
3) What determines the longitudinal stability of an aircraft?

Basic Empty Mass and Centre of Gravity

The ability to work out the basic empty mass and centre of gravity of an aircraft quickly is very important for the exam; you can save vital seconds if you are very

---

Basic Empty Mass and Centre of Gravity Sample Questions

1) Moment arms are measured from a specific point to the body station where the mass is located. What is this point known as?
2) An aircraft has a gross mass of 4,800kg; the centre of gravity is at station 115.9. What will be the new position of the centre of gravity if 300kg is moved from station 35 to station 100?
3) What is the payload available for an aircraft that has a basic empty mass of 4,000kg, ramp fuel of 700kg, taxi fuel of 80kg and an identical take-off, landing and zero fuel mass of 5,000kg?

---

familiar with these subjects. The BEM is a very specific measurement, and you need to know exactly what it comprises. It is advisable to be confident in working in different units and using conversions. A common question will ask how the aircraft's BEM should be weighed and how often this must be done.

Specific Gravity

Also relevant to mass and balance is specific gravity, as the mass of fuel, oil and potable water on the aircraft must be calculated. In different temperatures, the density of these liquids will vary, changing the mass of the fluid.

The CRP-5 is a very useful tool for calculating both the mass of liquids and converting between masses. Again, plenty of practice in using the instrument will save lots of vital time in your exam.

Specific Gravity Sample Question

What is the mass of fuel that may be loaded into an aircraft if the maximum quantity of fuel that can be loaded into its tanks is 4,000 US gal and the specific gravity of the fuel is 0.80?

Loading and Limitations

An aircraft's all-up mass (AUM) is made up of various components, and the relationship between these values should be memorized.

To simplify matters for airlines, 'standard mass values' for passengers and their bags are given in JAR-OPS 1. Although being familiar with these values would be useful, in my exam and those of many of my colleagues, none of these figures was required. That said, there were questions on the regulations surrounding the use of the values.

An aircraft also has many other weight limits for structural purposes, such as maximum zero fuel mass (MZFM) and maximum landing mass (MLM). These cannot be changed due to varying conditions and must be accommodated. You may be asked about these, in which case, you will have to work with various different structural weights to calculate a potential take-off mass. Again, practising these questions is the key.

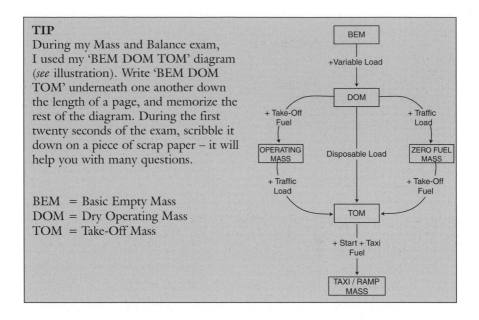

TIP
During my Mass and Balance exam, I used my 'BEM DOM TOM' diagram (*see* illustration). Write 'BEM DOM TOM' underneath one another down the length of a page, and memorize the rest of the diagram. During the first twenty seconds of the exam, scribble it down on a piece of scrap paper – it will help you with many questions.

BEM = Basic Empty Mass
DOM = Dry Operating Mass
TOM = Take-Off Mass

Loading and Limitations Sample Questions

1) The stalling speed will be highest when the aircraft is loaded with a centre of gravity in what position?
2) On short legs with minimum take-off fuel, for structural limitations, the traffic load is normally limited by which mass?
3) What are the reasons for ensuring that loads are adequately secured?

Cargo

When dealing with cargo, certain considerations must be taken into account. There will be a maximum mass limitation per hold, a maximum floor load per hold, a maximum volume per hold and a maximum running load. You will need to be able to calculate area loads – obviously, the larger an object's surface area, the lower its area load. To use a track or conveyor system, the running

---

Cargo Sample Question

1) The total mass of an aircraft is 8,000kg. The cg position is at 1.8m from the datum line. The aft limit for the cg is at 2.15m from the datum line. What mass of cargo must be shifted from the front cargo hold (at 0.9m from the datum) to the aft hold (at 3.5m) to move the cg to the aft limit?

TIP

I found that the key to success in Mass and Balance was practice, practice and more practice, together with the 'BEM TOM DOM' chart and memorizing the following five formulas:

1) *Load addition*

$$\frac{(\text{aircraft mass} \times \text{arm}) + (\text{load mass} \times \text{arm})}{\text{new total mass}}$$

2) *Load removal*

$$\frac{(\text{aircraft mass} \times \text{arm}) - (\text{load mass} \times \text{arm})}{\text{new total mass}}$$

3) *Load shift to give required cg position*

$$\frac{\text{distance cg needs to be moved} \times \text{aircraft total mass}}{\text{distance between the two holds}}$$

4) *Load removal or addition to give a required cg position*

$$\frac{\text{distance cg needs to be moved} \times \text{aircraft total mass}}{\text{distance between required cg and load}}$$

5) *Change in position of cg*

$$\frac{\text{mass shifted} \times \text{distance mass shifted}}{\text{aircraft total mass}}$$

load must be calculated and compared to the manufacturer's running-load limit. (Note that running load can also be called linear load.) You should also have a good understanding of the methods for securing cargo and the implications of it not being secured properly!

JAR-OPS

Mass and balance are dealt with in JAR-OPS, sub-part J. You must be familiar with this document for the exam. It contains information on the following items:

- Weighing an aircraft
- Use of 'fleet masses'
- Weighing procedure
- Aircraft loading
- Fuel density values
- Standard masses
- Documentation

JAR-OPS Sample Questions

1) What is the standard mass for a child?
2) How many seats are required before standard masses can be used for the computation of mass values of baggage?
3) How many points of support are required to measure the mass and centre of gravity of an aircraft?

PRINCIPLES OF FLIGHT

I found POF an interesting and enjoyable subject, albeit one of the most challenging of the course, and the one to which I had to allocate most of my study time. If you have some experience of aerospace engineering, such as a university degree, this is where it will come in useful, especially if you have studied aerodynamics. POF looks at what makes the aircraft fly, the limitations of flight and how lift is created. It would be very hard to pass this exam simply by learning facts, which you can do in some of the other subjects. You really need to get involved and have a thorough understanding of the principles. I will separate POF into the following areas:

- Measurement, Terminology and Lift
- Drag
- Propellers
- Flying Controls
- Climbing, Descending, Turning and Gliding
- Stalling
- Stability
- Asymmetric Flight
- Flight Limitations
- High-Speed Flight

Measurement, Terminology and Lift
Knowledge of the units of measurement and aircraft terminology (including V-speeds) is essential to make studying the rest of the syllabus easy. It is very important to be conversant with the Système Internationale (SI) units and know how to use them, as they will crop up in all of the work you will do in POF, together with the exam questions. In the Meteorology syllabus, you will have learned about the flight environment, and you will need to use aspects of this knowledge in your study of POF, such as the effect of altitude on temperature, density and pressure. Aircraft terminology must also be understood; if you have no flying experience and this is new, the best way to learn aircraft terminology is to go out on to the apron with an instructor or a labelled diagram of the aircraft and discover it for yourself. You should take a very close look at the wing and make sure you understand the different terms for its dimensions, such as 'chord', 'aspect ratio' and 'fineness ratio'. While looking around the aircraft, examine the pitot tube for both POF and Instruments

---

Measurement, Terminology and Lift Sample Questions

1) What is the SI unit of density?
2) What are the ISA values of pressure, density and temperature?
3) What is the term for a line from the leading edge of the wing to the trailing edge, equidistant from the upper and lower surface?
4) What is the term for the angle between the chord line of an aerofoil and the longitudinal axis?
5) If an aircraft has a wingspan of 9m and a wing area of 92sq.ft, what is the aspect ratio?
6) To obtain EAS from IAS, for what factors must corrections be made?
7) At a given TAS, what effect will an increase in air density have on lift?
8) To what speed does 'Vno' refer?

---

syllabuses. For the former, you will need to know how the pitot tube measures speed, and what speeds are calculated/measured for the aircraft's reference speed, such as its landing speed and stalling speed.

A thorough understanding of lift is absolutely essential to the rest of the POF syllabus, so make sure you have no doubts about it before continuing. Bernoulli's theorem may come up in the exam, so you must know the basic lift equation. The pressure of the airflow around an aerofoil should be known and will help you understand lift. This leads on to studying angle of attack and the effect of the airflow on this angle. The centre of pressure, centre of gravity and aerodynamic centre are all very different points on an aerofoil that are important in this syllabus; take care to understand and not to confuse them.

Various different shapes of wing will be studied, and you will need to know their basic characteristics and effects on lift. A wing can be swept back, up (dihedral) or down (anhedral), and all change the wing's properties, so they must be learned. The relationship between angle of attack and airspeed is a very important consideration; the graph that displays this relationship must be memorized, as it will be the subject of questions throughout the ATPL syllabus.

Drag

There are many different types of drag that affect aircraft, and they all cost airlines money. Each type of drag will be studied in detail, and it is very important to have a thorough understanding of them all. Perhaps the most important point to appreciate, however, is the relationship between induced drag and parasite drag, which will occur on many occasions throughout your course. It is also worth learning the drag equation, so that you know the factors that affect it and what happens to drag when one of the factors changes. Just as the wing shape will be studied for its effect on lift, so you will look at its effect on drag. You will also be questioned on how drag can be reduced by altering the aircraft's components. This is done by modifying the wing in a variety of ways, such as adding wing tips and washout, and tapering the wing. An understanding of how these methods reduce drag may prove useful.

Notice the lift and drag
devices used on this wing.

Drag Sample Questions

1) What is the purpose of a wing fence?
2) For a rectangular wing at a constant speed and angle of attack, what will happen to induced drag?
3) Where on the wing is interference drag created?
4) If the weight of an aircraft is increased, at a given speed, what will happen to the induced drag?
5) Which type of drag will lowering the undercarriage affect?
6) How can the wing shape be changed to decrease induced drag?
7) What is the approximate maximum lift/drag ratio of a typical transport aircraft?
8) If the weight of an aircraft is decreased, what will happen to the maximum lift/drag ratio?
9) In the accompanying illustration, show the point of minimum total drag.

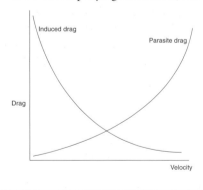

The lift/drag ratio is a way of expressing the drag penalty for any given amount of lift. The most efficient aircraft will create the most lift for the least drag. Every aircraft also has its most efficient speed, at which the least drag is produced. You will be questioned on this in many ways, so you need to

> **TIP**
> The blade face is the side that faces you when sitting in the cockpit.

have a very good understanding of the drag-against-IAS graph, showing both induced and parasite drag. Polar diagrams are used to indicate the relationship between the coefficient of lift and the coefficient of drag, and you should be familiar with using them for the exam.

Propellers

Power from an engine is converted into thrust by a propeller, and these devices may crop up not only in the POF exam, but also the AGK exam. Propeller terminology should be learned, and you can reinforce this by labelling a picture of a propeller (trailing edge, leading edge, shank, tip, blade angle and plane of rotation, blade face and blade back).

Just like a wing, a propeller has an angle of attack, and it is important to know the factors that affect this angle; it is worthwhile knowing how to draw a vector diagram of the angle, as that will help you to answer exam questions quickly and accurately. Remember that the propeller blade is just an aerofoil, exactly like a wing – it has a spanwise distribution of airflow that affects thrust, and it suffers from drag, such as tip vortices, like a wing. The pitch of the propeller is subject to change, and there are two different types of pitch: geometric and effective. The definitions of these must be known, as they are common questions. The propeller rotates at very high speeds and, as a result, is subjected to many different forces. Centrifugal force, thrust bending, aerodynamic turning moments (ATM), torque bending and centrifugal turning moments (CTM) all apply stresses to the propeller blade, so you will need to know the effects they have.

When you start flying in a single-engine piston aircraft, you will notice that it wants to swing to one side on take-off. The propeller creates many effects during this phase of flight, all of which need to be understood. They are torque effect, slipstream effect, gyroscopic effect and asymmetric blade effect.

Propellers Sample Questions

1) What will happen to the blade angle of attack if the RPM of a fixed-pitch propeller is increased while maintaining a constant airspeed?
2) What happens to propeller efficiency as you increase the number of propeller blades?
3) If a propeller turns to the right, as seen from behind, which way will the aircraft yaw due to the asymmetric thrust effect in the climb?
4) On a constant-speed propeller, as the speed increases, what happens to the blade angle?
5) What is the effect of centrifugal turning moments on a propeller's angle of attack?

Flying Controls

When familiarizing yourself with your aircraft, make sure you take a good look at the flying controls and the control surfaces, including the trim tabs and flaps. You need to know how the ailerons roll the aircraft, the different types of aileron (adverse yaw, differential and frise) and their characteristics. For the elevator, you should know about variable incidence and the all-moving tailplane, while for the rudder, you will need to be familiar with its purpose and the effects of its use. On some aircraft (such as the Concorde), the primary flying controls are combined to produce one control that is capable of two purposes. For example, the ailerons and flaps may be combined to produce 'flaperons'. You will need to know the possible control combinations, as you may be asked questions on them. Flying controls, especially on large aircraft, may be too heavy for the pilot to move unaided, so various methods of assisting the pilot are employed, such as aerodynamic balances, inset hinges or horn balances. Again, you must have an appreciation of these for the exam. A tab is used to balance the load acting on a control surface. There are many different types, and the advantages and disadvantages of each must be known. A very common exam question concerns aerodynamic flutter, which is caused by the pressure distribution around a control surface; you will need to know how that flutter is eliminated. Trim tabs may be movable or stationary, and you need to be aware of why each is used.

The different types of flap (such as Fowler, Kreuger, drooped leading edge, slotted and plain), their characteristics and the effect they have on the coefficient of lift must be understood. Flaps affect the take-off run and the angle of climb, and depending on the conditions, a decision will be made on whether or not to use them on take-off. You should be able to explain what effects the flaps have on this phase of flight and why you would elect to use them. When you start flying, you will be able to test the effects of flaps in straight and level flight and during the approach. This will really help your understanding, so if possible try to do this before taking the exam.

Flying Controls Sample Questions

1) When a leading-edge flap is extended, what happens to the coefficient of lift and the centre of pressure?
2) If a flapless landing must be made, what will happen to the landing speed?
3) What phenomenon is prevented by differential ailerons?
4) On an aircraft fitted with a servo tab, if the elevator became jammed, what would be the effect of the servo tab?
5) What happens to the length of the take-off run if you increase the normal flap setting for take-off?
6) Which control surface gives longitudinal control?
7) What is an elevon?

Climbing, Descending, Turning and Gliding

Unless an aircraft is flying straight and level, it will be climbing, descending, turning or gliding. The last is not an unusual occurrence; a large jet, for example, may spend the whole of its descent for around thirty minutes with the engines at idle, gliding to its destination.

An aircraft can climb at most speeds within its operating range, but there are two common climbing speeds that will be very important for the exam: Vx (speed for maximum angle of climb) and Vy (speed for maximum rate of climb). You will need to know the formulas for these speeds. You must also know the forces and vector diagrams for the aircraft when in a climb, turn, descent or glide, so try to learn them early on. You should have an appreciation of the factors that do (and do not) affect the climb and glide performance, such as headwind, flaps and weight. An additional consideration for gliding is how far the aircraft can glide, which is affected by the lift/drag ratio. Exam questions often give you the lift/drag ratio and an altitude, then ask you for a gliding distance.

Turning affects induced drag, and the consequences of this must be known. It also increases the load factor and changes the stalling speed due to the increase in lift required, so you will need to be familiar with the formulas for calculating these. Not all aircraft are capable of turning at any radius, so you must know how to work out an aircraft's radius of turn. This can be altered by various factors, such as flaps and altitude, which you will need to learn. Balancing the turn is important for comfort and aerodynamic efficiency; if the turn is not balanced, slipping or skidding will occur. You will learn about this in your initial flying training and will appreciate how important it is. This practical experience will help you to picture what a skidding or a slipping turn looks and feels like.

Climbing, Descending, Turning and Gliding Sample Questions

1) During a steady climb, what relationship is the lift force compared to the weight force?
2) Compared to still air, when gliding into a headwind, how will the ground distance covered change?
3) What is the percentage increase in stall speed in a 45° banked turn?
4) What would happen to the range of the aircraft during a glide if the weight decreased?
5) What conditions are required for a skidding turn?
6) In a steady level turn, what will happen to the radius of turn if the aircraft weight increases?

TIP
To find the angle required for a Rate 1 turn, take the speed (e.g. 180kt) and remove the last digit (18), then add seven to that number (25°).

> **TIP**
> As a rough guide, any percentage change in weight will produce approximately half the percentage change in stalling speed.

Stalling

The subject of stalling is quite complex and requires a lot of study. Having a good understanding of the concepts of centre of pressure and centre of gravity will be useful. You need to know the critical angle of attack for an average aircraft and be aware of the factors that affect it. You also need an appreciation of the factors that affect the stalling speed and to be familiar with the formulas for calculating these changes. (The factors include weight, configuration, power and manoeuvres.)

The ability to recognize the stall is essential, and you may be asked questions about this, such as how a stall warning system operates in both light and heavy aircraft. As with lift and drag, various wing shapes affect stalling characteristics, so you will need to know these. Stalling, including that of the wing tip, can be alleviated by the use of stick pushers, aerodynamic modifications such as washout, wing fences and vortex generators, all of which could come up in the exam. You will also need an appreciation of the deep stall, which can affect swept-back wings and T-tailed aircraft. A deep stall is very dangerous, and aircraft that are susceptible to this effect must be fitted with stall prevention systems. Finally, spinning (a stalled condition) should be studied. In the exam, you may be asked how the position of the centre of gravity affects an aircraft's spin characteristics.

Stalling Sample Questions

1) What is the standard stall recovery for a light aircraft?
2) When entering a stall, what happens to the centre of pressure in a swept-wing aircraft?
3) What effect do slats have on the stalling angle of attack?
4) What would the stalling speed be for an aircraft with a 1g stalling speed of 60kt IAS during a 60° turn?
5) What happens to lift and drag as the aircraft is pitched above the stalling angle?
6) How does the stall speed (IAS) vary with altitude?
7) Which aircraft design is the most likely to suffer from super stall?

Stability

Aircraft stability is a very large subject, which can seem quite daunting at first. As your understanding of it develops, however, it should gradually become easier. In the exam, there are likely to be quite a few questions from this section, so if you can obtain a good grasp of the subject, they offer the potential for easy marks. The key to understanding this subject is to ensure that you understand the concept of neutral, static and dynamic stability. It would be

---

Stability Sample Questions

1) If an aircraft has static directional stability and it sideslips to the right, which way will it yaw/roll?
2) What is the distance between the cg and the neutral point called?
3) In what way will lateral stability be affected by wings with sweep-back?
4) To provide the required manoeuvre stability, an aircraft in straight and level flight requires a stick force of 150lb/g. If n = 2.5, what is the increase in stick force required?
5) What effect will increased geometric dihedral have on lateral stability and dutch roll?
6) The fin provides directional stability about which axis?
7) What will happen to an aircraft that has neutral stability after a disturbance?
8) The pendulous effect of a high-winged aircraft improves what kind of stability?

---

very difficult to cover all the aspects of stability in this book, so I shall leave that to the classroom! Suffice to say, you need an understanding of all the factors affecting stability and the effects caused by movement of the centres of gravity and presure. The aspects of stability that should be covered are:

- Longitudinal static stability
- Longitudinal dynamic stability
- Lateral/directional dynamic stability
- Lateral static stability
- Directional static stability
- Stick-force stability
- Manoeuvre stability

Asymmetric Flight
Once you have completed your single-engine flying, you will move on to the twin. Do not get used to relying on two engines, though, because for most of the time you will be experiencing asymmetric flight on only one! You might think that the most important aspect about an engine failure in a twin is that less power is available, but you also have to deal with a yawing moment and a lot of drag. You will need to learn the exact definition of the single-engine inoperative speeds, such as Vmca, Vmcg and Vmcl, as they are likely to come up in at least one of your exams. Asymmetric blade effect can increase the yawing moment, and it is worse if you are faced with failure of the 'critical engine' – you will need to know the definition of this. Asymmetric flight is also affected by other factors, such as weight, rolling and turning. Lastly, and perhaps most importantly for your actual twin-engine flying, you must know how to recognize which engine has failed without reference to the engine instruments or looking at the engine itself.

Asymmetric Flight Sample Questions

1) Which would be the most critical engine to lose on a four-engine jet aircraft during take-off with a strong crosswind from the left?
2) How will Vmca be affected by having the undercarriage down?
3) Vmcl can be limited by:
   i) Engine failure during take off.
   ii) Maximum rudder deflection.
   Which of the above, if any, is correct?
4) Define the 'critical engine'.

Flight Limitations

The aircraft's manoeuvre envelope, which can be affected by adverse weather such as icing, will impose flight limitations. The JAA has laid down a minimum load limit requirement for both positive and negative load factors for different aircraft categories, all of which should be known. All aircraft are certified within a basic manoeuvre envelope, which limits the maximum and minimum speed and load factors. There are also design speeds (Va, Vb, Vc and Vd), and you must commit their definitions to memory. Gust factors must be taken into account for flight in turbulent conditions, and there is a JAR gust load factor envelope that indicates how aircraft speed should be limited depending on the gust factor. These figures should be memorized, as they may come up in exam questions.

Icing is probably the most dangerous of all weather conditions for an aircraft, so you must know the effects caused by contamination of the airframe, especially of the wing, flaps and slats. Take-off and landing performance will be reduced, and it may affect the point at which the stall warning system is activated; all of these aspects must be studied. The different types of wind shear (vertical, horizontal, updraught and downdraught) should also be understood, as should the effects they have on the aircraft. You must be conversant with the standard wind-shear recovery if it is encountered near the ground while landing. A microburst will endanger the aircraft by forcing it beyond its flight limitations, so you need to know the effect of this phenomenon during an approach or take-off; you may study this in the Meteorology syllabus as well. There are systems to detect such adverse weather conditions,

---

Flight Limitations Sample Questions

1) How will a coating of hoar frost affect the aircraft's stalling speed?
2) What speed is represented on the manoeuvre envelope?
3) Define Vfe.
4) A horizontal wind shear results in a 20 per cent reduction in IAS. To what level will the aerodynamic forces of lift and drag be reduced?
5) What is the JAR positive limit load factor for utility aircraft?

> **TIP**
> If asked about the design of a high-speed aircraft, just consider the extreme and think of the shape of the Concorde.

such as weather radar and passive infra-red radiometry, and it would be worthwhile knowing a little about them.

High-Speed Flight

This subject is not restricted purely to aircraft capable of travelling faster than the speed of sound. On occasion, some of the air flowing around an aircraft that is cruising much slower, say Mach 0.8, can reach the speed of sound. It is very important for both the POF and Instruments syllabuses that you are confident in using the formula for the Mach number and the local speed of sound. It is also essential that you absorb from the Instruments syllabus the factors that affect the Mach number as you travel through different parts of the atmosphere. You will need a good understanding of various types of Mach number, such as detachment, free stream and critical. You must have an appreciation of compressibility and shockwave formation, and how the latter move across the wing's surface, together with their effect on drag and flight. When dealing with supersonic flow, more types of drag are relevant, such as interference, trim, energy and boundary-layer separation. Shock waves can also cause control problems that must be overcome, by means of powered flying controls and all-moving surfaces for example. 'Mach tuck' is another problem that must be studied in detail. It occurs when you accelerate through the transonic speed range, being generated by the shock waves causing a nose-down pitching moment and an increase in speed. You will need to know a little about the design features of an aircraft intended for high-speed flight, such as swept-back wings, small leading edges and supercritical wings.

You may be asked about the area rule, which is a design feature for mating different parts of an aircraft (smoothing out lumps). There are various methods of applying the area rule, and you must be familiar with them. The buffet boundary graph may also come up in a question; it gives an acceptable speed range for given altitudes. Make sure you are familiar with its use and the factors that affect it.

High-Speed Flight Sample Questions

1) At a speed approaching Mach 1.0, where would you expect to see a shockwave first?
2) As air flows through a shockwave, what happens to its speed?
3) What will happen to the critical Mach number when a control surface is deflected down?
4) Is it acceptable for a transport aircraft to exceed the Mach buffet onset speed?
5) What happens to the Mach buffet margin as you increase altitude?
6) What wing characteristic would be best to increase the critical Mach number?
7) What is the reason for an aircraft having a 'Coke-bottle-shaped' fuselage?

Chapter 6
Ground School –
Phase Two

After sitting an exhausting and challenging set of exams, it was not long before I had another armful of books and folders that would prepare me for the second batch of exams. Having experienced the level of work required and realizing that I was capable of passing the exams, I started Phase Two with a much more confident attitude, which helped me throughout. Phase Two was a little different in that it consisted of a day in ground school followed by a day flying. This provided a much needed variation in day-to-day life, while flying every other day was a great motivator.

Unlike Phase One, the work began immediately on the first day. A good knowledge of many aspects of aviation was expected, since we had already studied them during the first part of the course. Although the new subjects were no easier, they were slightly different in that most of them did not require a deep understanding of concepts. Instead, many items had to be memorized, such as tables of numbers.

As in Chapter 5, I will give a breakdown of each subject in Phase Two, together with my thoughts and experiences, helpful tips and exam techniques, plus any other relevant details.

PERFORMANCE

Performance was not one of my favourite subjects. You will need to call on knowledge gained from the other syllabuses before you start, such as Meteorology, Operational Procedures, Mass and Balance, and mostly Principles of Flight. The exams concern some of the following aspects of performance, but most of the questions I was given were linked very closely to Principles of Flight. This subject covers performance for jet and piston aircraft during take-off, in the cruise, on landing and in the go-around. You will be issued with a *CAP 698* publication, which you will use in the exam, as it contains essential graphs. The Performance syllabus can be broken down into the following areas:

- Take-Off Performance
- Take-Off Weight and Speed
- Other Take-Off Procedures

- Class A Flight Performance
- Class B Flight Performance
- Flight for Range and Endurance

Take-Off Performance

A landing strip has different sections that must be considered in take-off calculations. These are the runway itself, the clearway and the stop-way. You will need to know the definitions of these areas and the calculations used to determine whether an aircraft can take off in the space available. There are JAR safety factors that must be added to the distances calculated, so you must have a thorough understanding of them – some exam questions may be framed to catch you out if there is any ambiguity over whether or not they should be applied.

Decision speeds are vital aspects of the take-off procedure and relate to the runway length. Once you reach a particular calculated speed, you must continue the take-off, as there will not be enough runway left to stop. You must be fully conversant with all of these take-off speeds.

There are other factors that also must be considered for the take-off, such as runway slope and wind components. You will need to dig into your Meteorology knowledge, as the pressure altitude, temperature and density altitude will have an effect on take-off. One other calculation that may be required of you in the exam concerns the aircraft and pavement classification numbers. These must be considered to ensure that the runway and taxiways can support the weight of the aircraft.

TIP
The *CAP 698* publication includes the take-off distance factors that you will need, so there is no need to memorize them. However, you do need to know where to find them.

Take-Off Performance Sample Questions
1) What components comprise the acceleration stop distance available (ASDA)?
2) What is the definition of a 'frangible obstacle'?
3) What would happen if the pilot were to abort the take-off run after V1?
4) The elevation of an airport is 2,600ft AMSL, the QNH is 1014 with ISA temperature. What is the density height of the airport?
5) What is the runway slope of runway 09 if it is 900m long, the threshold of runway 27 is 300ft and the threshold of runway 09 is 149ft?

Take-Off Weight and Speed

Questions about take-off weight and speed often occur in the exam, requiring the use of the graphs in *CAP 698*. Many different limits can be calculated

TIP
Factors Affecting Take-Off Speed

Factor	V1	Vr	V2	Vmcg	Vmca
Increased take-off mass	I	I	I		
Increased pressure altitude					
or temperature	I	I	D	D	D
Increased flap	D	D	D		
Increased upslope	I				
Increased headwind	I				
I = increases D = decreases					

from the graphs, such as tyre, brake energy and structural limits. To produce accurate answers quickly, you will need plenty of practice in using the graphs. Sometimes, the multiple-choice answers given in the exam are so close together that it is very difficult to decide between them, and accuracy is the key to success.

Many different reference speeds are used for take-off, all of which are denoted by abbreviations. You will need to become familiar with all of these and understand the relationships between them. A very common exam question will give you a speed, such as V1, Vr or V2, and ask you what will happen to it if a factor changes, for example, the pilot deciding to use more flap on take-off. It is possible to produce a table of effects and memorize the results (*see* Factors Affecting Take-Off Speed), but it is better if you can understand the factors and possess the ability to calculate the results.

Take-Off Weight and Speed Sample Questions
1) In *CAP 698*, Figure 4.4, why is there a correction made for engine anti-icing, but not for wing anti-icing?
2) Which speed represents the maximum value for V1, assuming maximum tyre speed and maximum brake energy speed are not limiting?
3) What is the meaning of the speed Vmu?
4) What is the effect of a decrease in temperature on Vr?
5) If the wind sheared during take-off and became more of a tailwind, what would happen if you aborted the take-off at the calculated V1?

Other Take-Off Procedures
If you take a look through *CAP 698*, you will see that it gives other take-off procedures. These include reduced-thrust take-offs to save money, improved obstacle clearance and take-offs from contaminated runways. You will need to familiarize yourself with all of these procedures and their associated graphs, as you may be asked questions about them. The definition of a contaminated runway is also a common question, both in this subject and in Operational Procedures, so you should know the precise definition. Noise abatement is a

---

Other Take-Off Procedures Sample Questions

1) Using the increased V2 technique, which speeds are increased when compared to a normal take-off?
2) Given a tyre pressure of 10 bar, at what speed is there a risk of dynamic aquaplaning?
3) How much of the runway's surface area must be covered by the critical depth of water, slush or snow for it to be considered contaminated?
4) Refer to *CAP 698*, Figure 4.14. What is the maximum permitted take-off mass with a pressure altitude of 2,500ft, temperature of +10°C, field length of 6,500ft, field length limited take-off mass of 54,000kg and 13mm of standing water?
5) In what conditions would a runway be described as damp?

---

topic that is becoming increasingly more important as air travel grows, and two procedures are normally used to prevent excessive noise. One reduces noise close in to the airport, while the other prevents excessive noise in areas farther away; you will need an understanding of both.

Class A Flight Performance
The take-off for a Class A aircraft is split into four segments, the specific definitions of which must be known. For each of the four segments, there are climb gradients that must be achieved, and these must be committed to memory, together with the corrections for an engine failure. There are also regulations regarding turns after take-off – turns can only be made in certain segments and there is a minimum obstacle clearance that must be maintained. Obstacle clearance on take-off is a factor to consider, particularly if the runway has a downward slope. If you start a take-off on a downward sloping runway, the height of an object at the end of the runway will effectively grow, so you will need to know how to calculate this change given a slope gradient.

The performance of an aircraft en-route must be considered, so you will need to know the definition of the en-route phase. There are en-route obstacle clearances to take into account and other clearances if an engine fails. If the latter occurs at high altitude on a twin-engine aircraft, a drift down will be made. It is important that you understand the drift-down principle, as you will need it later in the ATPL course. Suitably certified twin-engine aircraft can fly over areas where there are very few suitable airfields for landing. This is called extended-range operations (EROPS). You will need an appreciation of the performance considerations for EROPS flights, and to know the difference between an 'adequate' and a 'suitable' airfield.

The landing phase is also subject to performance regulations, so you will need to be aware of the point at which the landing phase starts. The distance that the aircraft requires to come to a stop on the runway will need a safety factor adding to it, depending on the aircraft type. These safety

---

Class A Flight Performance Sample Questions

1) At what point does the second segment of the take-off commence?
2) What is the minimum height of flap retraction above reference zero?
3) What are the gross and net gradient requirements for a Class A aircraft in the third segment of take-off?
4) What is the safety factor applied to a jet aircraft to obtain the net landing distance on a wet runway?
5) After an engine failure, a twin-engine aircraft is unable to maintain its altitude. What is the procedure that must be applied?
6) When does an 'adequate' airport become 'suitable'?

---

factors must be committed to memory, since they are common questions. In the event of a go-around (missed approach), there are minimum climb gradients and minimum speeds that must be maintained; these will be studied. There may be questions on any of the landing charts in *CAP 698*, so it is well worth familiarizing yourself with these and practising frequently. There are instructions for each of the graphs, and it is better to read them before taking the exam.

Class B Flight Performance
The aircraft that you will fly during your ATPL training are likely to fall into Class B. When determining performance, you will need to consider many of the same factors that apply to Class A aircraft, and you will have to familiarize yourself with the appropriate regulations in *CAP 698*. You will need an appreciation of the factors that affect take-off, en-route and landing performance. With a single-engine Class B aircraft, if the engine fails, you will be in a gliding situation, so you will need to be aware of the laws regarding a glide. You will also need to know the definition of a service ceiling. A typical exam question concerning landing performance will ask you to find the maximum possible landing weight, given such factors as slope, runway surface, landing distance available, pressure altitude and wind component. Consequently, you will need to be very familiar with *CAP 698*.

For a multi-engine Class B aircraft, you will need an appreciation of the same regulations as for multi-engine Class A aircraft, but there will be some differences. For example, rather than an engine being assumed to fail at take-off, it is assumed to fail upon entering cloud. The regulations concerning this

---

TIP
When reading questions in the exam, beware of any that ask for dispatch/planned performance. In this case, you must use the most favourable runway, no headwind and an ISA temperature. Do not let this catch you out.

Class B Performance Sample Questions

1) Assuming a cloud base of 1,000ft and a net all-engines operating gradient of 11 per cent, what is the horizontal distance required from the end of the take-off distance to reach a height of 1,000ft above the aerodrome?
2) In *CAP 698*, Figure 3.9, what is the gross landing distance, taking into account the following conditions: pressure altitude 1,500ft, weight 4,100lb, temperature 5°C, wind 8kt head, runway slope level?
3) If the take-off distance required on a paved, dry runway is 3,200ft, what is the take-off distance required on a dry grass runway with the same weather conditions?
4) Assuming that control requirements are satisfied, how much above the stall speed should you be when passing the screen height?
5) A single-engine aircraft has a lift-to-drag ratio of 11:1 at its gliding speed. What is its net gradient of descent for the purpose of assessing the en-route performance after an engine failure?

are confusing, so I advise you to look into it very thoroughly. The en-route phase also differs slightly to that of a Class A aircraft, so be warned.

Flight for Range and Endurance

There are several aspects to flight for range and endurance, which looks at various factors of aircraft efficiency. You will need to memorize the formula for specific air range (SAR) and be able to use drag vs. velocity graphs, knowing where the maximum range and endurance points are located. You must have an appreciation of the factors that affect the best range and endurance speeds, such as altitude, temperature and wind. You will also need a knowledge of other cruise speeds, such as the minimum-cost cruise, highest-speed cruise and longest-range cruise, and understand how they affect other factors. Piston aircraft will be studied in the same way, but beware of the subtle differences between these and jets. For example, the drag vs. velocity graphs are slightly different, so try to find a way of remembering which is which for the exam. The final point about the Performance syllabus is that you really do need a good knowledge of the principles of

Flight for Range and Endurance Sample Questions

1) What would happen to endurance if the flaps were lowered?
2) As altitude increases, what happens to the power required to maintain a constant indicated airspeed?
3) What is the formula for specific air range?
4) What happens to the maximum range if the wing's aspect ratio is increased?
5) As an aircraft's wing loading increases, what happens to the maximum endurance, and does this occur at a higher or a lower speed?

flight. Although there were many questions on aircraft performance, I found that lots were related to the POF syllabus, so a good revision of it beforehand is worthwhile.

INSTRUMENTS

The Instruments syllabus is large; I studied it over the two phases and took the exam during Phase Two. It was an enjoyable subject, probably because it is linked directly to flying an aircraft, and it helped me understand the instruments that I was using every day to fly. It includes all the flight instruments found in light aircraft, together with the more advanced instrumentation employed in modern jet aircraft. Some of the syllabus was quite challenging, as the material was completely new to me, but I found that the exam was not as complicated as the material I had studied. Instruments can be broken down into the following subject areas:

- Pressure instruments
- Air Temperature, Angle of Attack and Air Data Systems
- Radio Altimeter
- Gyroscopic Instruments
- Magnetism and Compasses
- Inertial Navigation Systems (INS)
- Flight Management Systems (FMS)
- Automatic Flight Control Systems
- Engine Instruments
- Warnings and Recording Systems

Pressure Instruments
You will be using pressure instruments throughout your flying training, and they will be fitted in all the aircraft that you will fly, even the most modern of airliners. There are lots of questions on pressure instruments not only in the Instruments syllabus, but also in the Meteorology syllabus, where they take the form of altimetry questions. As in most other subjects, you will need to know all about the International Standard Atmosphere (ISA) and how it changes with altitude. Pitot and static pressure will be studied, and you must understand the principles of the pitot and static tubes, the altimeter (including servo-assisted types) and the vertical speed indicator (including instantaneous

> **TIP**
> An easy way to remember what happens to an airspeed indicator, if either the pitot or the static tube becomes blocked in a climb or descent, is to use the mnemonic POC SUC.
> Pitot blocked = Over-reads in a Climb
> Static blocked = Under-reads in a Climb

TIP

The components of the Mach meter are linked in a specific manner, and a common exam question asks for this link. I found that an easy way to remember it was by reciting the following sentence:

'The RAT RAN IN'.

The RATio arm is connected to the RANging arm, which is connected to the INstrument.

Pressure Instruments Sample Questions

1) What would happen to the airspeed reading if, during a descent, the pitot head became blocked?
2) What kind of pressure does a pitot head measure?
3) What does the upper limit of the green arc mean on the airspeed indicator?
4) What correction must be made to obtain CAS from IAS?
5) Which errors of an altimeter increase as altitude increases?
6) What is the purpose of the D-spring on a servo-assisted altimeter?
7) What is the purpose of the dashpot on an instantaneous vertical speed indicator?
8) When descending at a constant CAS below the tropopause in an ISA, what happens to the TAS and Mach number?
9) When flying at a constant Mach number and flight level from a warm to a cold air mass, what will happen to CAS and the true altitude?

---

versions), together with their limitations and errors. It is also well worth revising how to convert from indicated airspeed to true airspeed on your CRP-5. You must be able to read an airspeed indicator and know the meanings of the coloured markings.

You will study the Mach meter, so a knowledge of the speed of sound, how to calculate it and the factors that affect it will be very important. The way in which the Mach number is measured must be known, and you will learn how it is displayed on an instrument; you will need to know what errors affect the instrument.

The relationship between Mach number, true airspeed and calibrated airspeed is a vital part of the Instruments exam. In the exam I sat, almost 20 per cent of the questions concerned this relationship. There are various ways of learning the relationship, but I found the easiest was to memorize the formulas that link them and make any necessary adjustments. If you are not very good at manipulating formulas, however, there is a graph that can be sketched to help answer the questions.

Air Temperature, Angle of Attack and Air Data Systems

The measurement of air temperature is not as simple as it sounds; different temperatures can be measured, such as static, ram and total. You must know the differences between them. A common exam question will ask you to

---

Air Temperature, Angle of Attack and Air Data Systems Sample Questions

1) What is the formula for temperature error due to ram rise?
2) For what must total air temperature measured from an aircraft be corrected to obtain the static air temperature?
3) What does an air data computer use to measure an aircraft's altitude?

---

correct an error due to heating (ram rise), requiring you to use a specific formula. Modern airliners are usually equipped with angle-of-attack sensors, which are linked to computers and used for stall and wind-shear detection. You will need to understand their principle of operation, uses and errors.

Air data systems will also be studied, although I cannot recall any questions on them in the exam. All the instruments studied so far feed into an air data computer (ADC), which corrects for the various errors before sending more accurate information to the electronic displays.

Radio Altimeter

The radio altimeter is fitted to all modern airliners, and provides a much more accurate reading of height above the ground than a pressure altimeter. You will study how it works, how the information is displayed, the instrument's limitations and advantages, and the range in which it works.

Radio Altimeter Sample Questions

1) What frequency range does the radio altimeter use?
2) What is the range of a low-altitude radio altimeter?
3) What is the principle of operation of the radio altimeter?

Gyroscopic Instruments

To understand the operation of some aircraft instruments, it is necessary to have an appreciation of the properties of the gyroscope and how it works. I found gyroscopic principles quite a challenging subject to study, and in my exam, there were no questions relating to the devices.

The terminology surrounding gyros will have to be known, together with the ways in which they are powered (electrical or suction) and the benefits of each. Ring laser gyros are a development of the standard gyro, and you can expect questions on their principles, advantages and accuracy.

Directional gyroscopes are used as the basic heading references in light aircraft. They suffer from errors, however, such as real and apparent drift, and you must be aware of these. You will need to know how to compensate for apparent drift due to the Earth's rotation or to transport. There are formulas for calculating apparent drift and for the total drift suffered by a directional gyro; you should memorize these.

TIP

A good way to remember the properties of a gyroscope is to use the following sentence and table:

'I went to my GP; he told me to REST, then TAX'D me!'

Degrees of freedom	Gyro	Spin Axis	Properties
1	Rate	–	Turn indicator
2	Earth	|	Artificial horizon
3	Space	|	X
2	Tied	–	Directional gyro

For example, an Earth gyro has 2° of freedom, a vertical spin axis and is used in an artificial horizon.

TIP

A question that you can expect in the Instruments exam will ask what occurs during a turning error after so many degrees of turning. If you can memorize this table, you will find that you can answer the question very quickly and easily.

Degrees turned	Pitch illusion	Bank illusion
0	Correct	Correct
90	Over-pitch	Under-bank
180	Over-pitch	Correct
270	Over-pitch	Under-bank
360	Correct	Correct

The artificial horizon is the primary flight instrument used during Instrument flying. It employs a tied gyro, and you will need to know how it works, its properties and, of course, its problems. A development of the standard artificial horizon is the electrically powered artificial horizon, which you will also study. A knowledge of instrument errors will allow you to predict them in flight; they are common questions in the exam.

The turn-and-balance indicator is also important for instrument flying. If the aircraft is not balanced, this instrument will tell you if it is slipping or skidding. The principles of the indicator and its errors will need to be known. In addition, you should have an understanding of the rates of turn that the instrument displays, and how long it takes to turn through a given number of degrees at a specified rate of turn.

Magnetism and Compasses

I found magnetism and compasses another subject that took some time to understand fully. You will need a good knowledge of magnetism and its

---

Gyroscopic Instruments Sample Questions

1) What is the term for a gravity-controlled gyro that has gyroscopic inertia relative to the Earth's vertical?
2) For the most efficient gyroscope, where should the mass be concentrated?
3) What is the name of a gyro that has freedom in one plane in addition to the plane in which the rotor is spinning?
4) What are the most significant errors of a directional gyroscope?
5) A directional gyro in an aircraft is corrected to give zero drift when the aircraft is stationary on the ground at a latitude of 40°S. Assuming the gyro to be free of random wander, what change in gyro readings may be expected when the aircraft is stationary on the ground at 43°S?
6) In which instrument is a gravity erector system used to correct errors?
7) When an aircraft has turned through 270° with a constant attitude and bank, what does the pilot observe on the artificial horizon?
8) How many degrees of freedom does a turn indicator possess?
9) What is the relationship between the aircraft's TAS and the turn indicator reading in a turn at a constant rate?

---

properties, the Earth's magnetic field and all of the terminology involved. Much of it is also covered in the General Navigation syllabus.

An aircraft has magnetism as well, even though much of its structure is not magnetic, and some of its components can produce magnetic fields that may affect compass readings. These errors are compensated for by 'swinging' the compass, which you will need to understand. JAR requirements for compass installation and accuracy are covered in this syllabus.

The direct indicating compass is a simple device powered only by the Earth's magnetic field, and it will probably come up in the exam. You will need to know about its construction, design features and errors. The two types of error on which you are likely to be questioned are turning and acceleration errors. These will be demonstrated to you when you start instrument flying.

TIP

For acceleration errors that apply to a direct indicating compass in the Northern Hemisphere, memorize the following mnemonic:

ANDS (Accelerating causes apparent turn to North; Decelerating causes apparent turn to South.)

For turning errors in the Northern Hemisphere, memorize the following mnemonic:

UNOS (Undershoot if turning toward North; Overshoot if turning toward South.)

Magnetism and Compasses Sample Questions

1) At the magnetic Equator, what are the angle of dip and the angle of magnetic variation?
2) What is required to calculate the compass heading from the magnetic heading?
3) An aircraft in the Northern Hemisphere turns to the right from a heading of 340° magnetic at Rate 1. What is the compass likely to read after twenty seconds?
4) In the Southern Hemisphere, on what heading are acceleration errors greatest?
5) What does a slow oscillation of the annunciator mean on a remote indicating compass?
6) On a remote indicating compass, to what is the output of the flux valve fed?

The remote indicating compass is a more accurate compass system that employs a detector to sense the aircraft's heading relative to the Earth's magnetic field. Because the sensor is remote, it is less susceptible to interference from the aircraft's magnetism. The compass comprises various components, which you must understand. You will also need to know how it is operated, its errors and its limitations.

Inertial Navigation Systems

Used for self-contained navigation, inertial navigation systems are quite complicated. Basically, an INS uses accelerometers to calculate all the movements made by the aircraft, which are added to its initial position so that a new position can be calculated. The system does not require any other information, as it has a model of the Earth built into it. With the exception of a few errors, it is extremely accurate. You will need to know the two different methods of compensating for aircraft attitude change: 'strapping down' and 'stable platform'. One of the drawbacks of INS is that an initial position of the aircraft must be calculated, which takes some time. You will need an appreciation of how an INS unit is operated and what you can expect to see on a control display unit (CDU). The errors affecting the INS are either 'bounded' or 'unbounded'; you must have an understanding of these, as you may be asked to identify them in the exam.

Inertial Navigation Systems Sample Questions

1) What inputs must be made to the INS to correct for Earth rate and transport wander?
2) What type of error is caused by a Schuler loop oscillation of the stable platform in an INS?
3) What is the period of oscillation of a pendulum when disturbed?

Flight Management Systems

The FMS is commonly used in modern airliners. It is a navigational system that assists the pilot to fly an aircraft with maximum efficiency and safety. The device comprises various sub-systems, including auto-throttle, INS and an Electronic Flight Instrument System (EFIS). The FMS control display unit is important, and you are likely to be asked about the sequence of pages through which it runs.

Flight Management Systems Sample Questions

1) As what can the FMS be defined?
2) Why is it necessary to insert local geographical co-ordinates to align a 'strap-down' inertial unit?
3) What is the period of validity of the time-sensitive data stored in the permanent database in the FMS?
4) At what point of a flight is it most likely that navigation aids would provide the FMS with an inaccurate radio position?

Automatic Flight Control Systems

I found automatic flight control systems a challenging subject, but I think this was because I was unable to obtain any hands-on experience with them, unlike most other aspects studied during my flying training. There were not many questions on these systems in the exam, perhaps 5–10 per cent of the total, and the material covered in the lessons seemed much more complicated than that in the exam. You will need to know a little about the flight instruments and displays used by automatic flight control systems: the flight director, autopilot, auto-land, auto-throttle, yaw damper and fly by wire. I found that most questions concerned the symbols and colours that a pilot would see on the displays, such as what the colour coding means (red items indicate warning and amber items refer to cautions).

Automatic Flight Control Systems Sample Questions

1) What is the name for a closed-loop control system in which a small power input controls a much larger power output in a strictly proportionate manner?
2) If a pilot engages control-wheel steering (CWS) and carries out a manoeuvre in roll, what will the autopilot do when the controls are released?
3) What will the autopilot do if it is engaged without any modes selected?
4) The auto trim is a component of the autopilot pitch channel. What is its function?
5) What is the name of an automatic landing system in which the landing must be made manually if there is a system failure during the approach?

Engine Instruments

This is another subject area about which there were very few questions in the exam. You will study the different kinds of tachometer, together with pressure, torque, temperature, fuel flow, fuel contents and vibration measurement systems. You will need to know roughly how each works and the different variants. Three methods of measuring pressure are covered in the syllabus, and a common exam question will ask which method should be used for a given type of pressure.

Electronic displays are also used to give engine instrument information (Engine Indication and Crew Alerting System, EICAS). You will need to know what the EICAS is capable of displaying, together with the tasks of each of its two displays (primary and secondary).

Engine Instruments Sample Questions

1) What does a vibration meter measure?
2) What does a bellows measure?
3) Compared to a volumetric flow meter, for what does a mass flow meter compensate?
4) Some piston-engine aircraft have a red arc inside the green arc on the RPM gauge. Why should this red arc be avoided?
5) What would the contents gauge show for a fuel tank with a capacitive contents gauging system that had some water in it, but no fuel?
6) What is the purpose of a synchroscope?

Warnings and Recording Systems

I found studying warnings and recording systems to be quite enjoyable; it is not quite so technical as the other parts of the Instruments syllabus. On a modern airliner's flight deck, there are endless numbers of aural and visual warnings, so you will need to know the different types and their purposes. You must appreciate the difference between warnings, cautions and advisories, and know the meaning of each aural alert (bell, voice, siren and wailer). Sometimes, warnings are inhibited during critical stages of flight, such as the take-off, and you will need to be aware of the exact times when this occurs.

The ground proximity warning system (GPWS) alerts the crew when an aircraft is in a potentially dangerous situation and could hit the ground. You may need to know the inputs required for this system and the warnings it gives. There are standard voice warnings for the different types of alert, such as 'Sink rate' and 'Too low, terrain'. For each alert, you must be aware of the associated voice warning, the warning envelope, the flight hazard and the GPWS mode. A common exam question will ask which warnings are priorities, because if two occur, they must be prioritized.

Another system that will be studied is the traffic alert and collision avoidance system (TCAS). This will alert the pilot to other traffic in the vicinity and issue a warning if it poses a collision risk. You will need to understand the various symbols that are used to indicate the different threats from aircraft, and also know the limits of proximity before an aircraft does become a threat. Knowledge of the principle of operation of TCAS (Radar) and its limitations may also be required.

To aid accident investigation, some aircraft are required to carry recording systems. You will need to know the types of aircraft to which this requirement applies and the maximum period of time the equipment must be capable of recording. Exam questions may cover how the recorders should be stored on the aircraft and in what packaging, what the recorders do and do not record, and the length of time the recordings must be kept before deletion.

Warnings and Recording Systems Sample Questions

1) What is the regulatory margin between a stall warning and the stall speed?
2) Except for aircraft of less than 5.7 tonnes, for how long must a flight data recording system be able to store the recorded data?
3) According to ICAO Annex 6, part 1, where in the aircraft should the flight data recorder be located?
4) How is a 'close traffic advisory' displayed on a TCAS 2 system?
5) What kind of warnings must the over-speed warning system provide?
6) On a TCAS, what is the aural warning that accompanies 'traffic advisory'.
7) What does the GPWS annunciate when the aircraft has flaps down and an excessive rate of descent?

HUMAN PERFORMANCE AND LIMITATIONS (HPL)

Another subject that I enjoyed very much was Human Performance and Limitations. It is quite different from the other syllabuses that make up the course, in that it is not technical and has little to do with aircraft. If you can remember lots of your biology lessons from school, it will be advantageous. The subject is split into two areas, covering the physical and mental effects of flying. It is important because your career depends on your health and performance; it offers plenty of health advice to consider during your career. It also gives information on lots of the problems and hazards associated with regular flying. You will need a very good understanding of the make-up of the atmosphere and of the gas laws. You should have this knowledge already, as you will have studied these aspects extensively in most of the other subjects, especially Meteorology.

HPL can be split into the following subject areas:

- Basic Human Factors
- Respiratory and Circulatory Systems
- High Altitude

- Vision and Hearing
- Acceleration and Balance
- Other Physiological Problems
- Processing Information and Decision Making
- Personality and Stress
- Flight-Deck Design
- Sleep and Fatigue
- Learning
- Flight Safety

Basic Human Factors

This is a simple introduction to the medical requirements of a pilot and the frequency with which they should be checked. It also covers what happens if medical fitness falls for any reason, such as old age, sickness or pregnancy.

Basic Human Factors Sample Questions

1) If a pilot is sick, they should inform the authority if they have not recovered after how many days?
2) If a member of aircrew donates blood, how long must they wait before they are able to fly again?

Respiratory and Circulatory Systems

A good understanding of the body's respiratory and circulatory systems will prove useful, as the following sections on the problems of altitude build upon this. The function of respiration and its components will be studied, and you will need to know the various terms used for lung capacity and average breathing rates.

You will need an appreciation of the difference between tracheal air and alveolar air, and the concept of partial pressures. As you climb in altitude, the partial pressure of oxygen in the alveoli changes; you will need to know how it changes and the approximate values at different altitudes.

A good understanding of the heart and its functions is essential. You must know where the oxygenated and deoxygenated blood flows, the difference between arteries, veins and capillaries, and the output of the heart (cardiac output). Questions on blood pressure occur frequently; you will

---

TIP

You must be aware of the route that oxygen follows from breathing it in until it is absorbed by the blood. You can create a way of remembering this by using the following sentence:

'All The Best Beers Are Brown!' (Atmosphere, Trachea, Bronchi, Bronchioles, Alveoli, Bloodstream.)

> **TIP**
> Throughout this subject, you will come across words preceded by either 'hypo' or 'hyper'. The former refers to a small value, such as low pressure, whereas the latter refers to anything that has a high value, such as high blood pressure.

need an appreciation of typical values of blood pressure and the two different measures that are used.

Blood comprises different components, each of which has specific duties that you must understand. Heart diseases are also examined. You will need to know the different types and their associated causes (orthostatic hypotension, angina, infarct, heart attack, anaemia, stroke and circulatory shock).

Respiratory and Circulatory Systems Sample Questions

1) Which law refers to the total pressure of a mixture of gases being equal to the sum of the partial pressures of the gases that compose the mixture?
2) Is the partial pressure of carbon dioxide in the alveoli higher or lower than that in the blood?
3) What are the percentages of oxygen and carbon dioxide in the alveolar air at sea level?
4) What are the functions of the left and right ventricles of the heart?
5) What is the biggest factor that increases the risk of coronary heart disease?
6) What is the typical diastolic blood pressure of a healthy young person?

High Altitude

You will be spending the rest of your career at high altitudes, so it is important to learn about the effects this may produce. Probably the most studied problem is hypoxia, although hyperventilation has similar symptoms, so it is important to be able to differentiate between the two. You will need to know the different types of hypoxia and their causes, and for each you must be aware of the symptoms and signs. You will also study the factors that affect the onset of hypoxia, such as temperature, exposure and smoking. It is very important to memorize the time of useful consciousness (TUC) figures, as there is often a question on them. You will need to know the figures at rest and when active, for different altitudes. Also, different altitudes represent different stages, such as the compensatory stage (10,000–15,000ft), and for each of these stages, you must have an appreciation of the effects.

Hyperventilation is a significant effect of high altitude. You should know why it occurs, together with its signs and symptoms, which are very similar to hypoxia. A common exam question will give you a list of symptoms and ask you to choose between hypoxia and hyperventilation. You will also need to know how hyperventilation is treated.

You will study many other problems associated with flying at high altitudes in an air conditioned, pressurized cabin; you will need to know their causes and the problems associated with them. They include radiation, dehydration and rapid depressurization.

High Altitude Sample Questions

1) What symptom is common to both hyperventilation and hypoxia?
2) When flying at night, what is the first sense to be affected by hypoxia?
3) What is a comfortable relative humidity for most people?
4) What are the two types of radiation that can be experienced while airborne?
5) What is the cause of hyperventilation?

Vision and Hearing

The senses of vision and hearing are vital when flying an aircraft. You will make an extensive study of the eye, and will need to know all of its parts and their functions. You will also learn about the problems associated with the eye, such as blind spots, empty-field myopia and vision limitations. Perception will be covered as well, including how the eye measures depth or the size of something in the distance. You will be taught about eye correction and sunglasses, which will be useful when you come to select a good pair for yourself. You will need to know the difference between being long-sighted and short-sighted, how these conditions are corrected and other problems that may occur with the eye, such as colour blindness, glaucoma and hypo-glycaemia. Flying creates many visual illusions that affect such aspects as runway perspective, especially in bad weather. You must have an appreciation of these not only for the exam, but also for your own flying, as you are likely to come across such illusions often.

In addition, you must have a knowledge of the laws that apply to pilots and vision correction, such as the types of correction allowed and those that are not.

Study of the ear is determined by a very similar syllabus to that of the eye, in that you will need to know all of its parts and what they do, especially the outer, middle and inner ear. Noise intensity is measured in decibels, and you

---

TIP

I used the following sentence to remember the names of eye problems and how they are corrected:

'MY NEAR CAVE in LONG island!'

It translates as: MYopia is when you are NEAR-sighted, and you require a conCAVE lens to correct it. When you are LONG-sighted, the opposite applies (you need a convex lens).

> **Vision and Hearing Sample Questions**
> 1) How long does the eye need to adapt fully to the dark?
> 2) What type of scanning technique should you use when flying at night?
> 3) What can you do to prevent the auto-kinetic phenomena?
> 4) Why should you not fly when suffering from a cold?
> 5) To which part of the ear do the ossicles belong?
> 6) What can be done to relieve barotrauma of the middle ear?

must be aware of how many decibels it takes to damage your hearing or even rupture the ear drum. You will need an understanding of different types of hearing loss and how to protect your hearing.

Acceleration and Balance

You will look at the different axes of acceleration, and classify the different types of acceleration and balance sustained by an aircraft. Harnesses are employed to help you withstand acceleration, and you will need to be aware of the different types and their uses. Each type of acceleration has a different effect on your body; you will need an understanding of these effects and how they may affect your performance. The vestibular apparatus in the ear senses these accelerations, so you must have a knowledge of this and the limitations to which it is subject, such as vestibular illusions. Spatial disorientation can be a major problem when flying an aircraft, especially in bad weather. You must know how this illusion is caused and how to overcome it.

> **Acceleration and Balance Sample Questions**
> 1) How is air sickness caused and at what vibration frequency is it most common?
> 2) During flight in cloud, what is the most reliable sense that should be used to overcome illusions?
> 3) In which axis can the body tolerate short accelerations of up to 45g?
> 4) The vestibular apparatus senses what kind of accelerations?

Other Physiological Problems

You must be aware of several other physiological problems that could be caused by flying or affect your performance in the air. These include taking medication or alcohol, smoking, toxic materials (such as fuel vapour), carbon monoxide poisoning, tropical diseases, gastro-intestinal diseases picked up abroad, diseases from insects, hepatitis and incapacitation. You may be asked for the side-effects of certain medications, and you will need to know how you would be affected by different alcohol concentrations, together with the

---

Other Physiological Problems Sample Questions

1) What is the time of useful consciousness (TUC) after a rapid depressurization at 35,000ft when at rest?
2) Which disease is considered to be the world's biggest killer?
3) What is the best method of controlling your weight?
4) What is the most common cause of pilot incapacitation?
5) What is the difference between a faint and a fit?

---

definition of alcoholism. A considerable amount of time is spent studying smoking, as it has a significant adverse effect on most aspects of flying. You will need an appreciation of a variety of toxicants, especially aviation fuels and oils. Since you are likely to be travelling around the world throughout your career, tropical diseases caused by insects, water and food will be covered. Incapacitation need not mean death; it may be the result of severe food poisoning. You will need an understanding of the different types of incapacitation, their common causes and how it is detected.

Processing Information and Decision Making

You will need a basic understanding of how humans process information and store it in their memories. The two different types of memory – iconic and echoic – occur frequently in exam questions. You should also have some understanding of the working memory, the length of time that information can be stored, how many items of information can be stored and how these can be passed into the long-term memory. Situational awareness is a very important asset for a pilot, and you will need an appreciation of its different levels (monitor, evaluate and anticipate).

Decision making is an important task for the pilot. You will study how the decision-making process works – recognize the problem, gather information, formulate alternatives, evaluate the alternatives and feedback. Then, you will look at group decision making and compare it to individual decision making, considering the factors involved (ability, status and role).

Processing Information and Decision Making Sample Questions

1) In which memory are visual and auditory stimuli stored?
2) Which personality characteristic makes crew decision-making most effective?
3) How many items can usually be stored in the short-term memory?
4) With which memory is environmental capture associated?

Personality and Stress

You will study personality diagrams, plotting the level of a person's anxiety and extroversion on to a graph. This will put the person into one of four groups, each indicating a different type of personality. Behaviour is grouped by the Rasmussen model into skill based, rule based and knowledge based; you should know the characteristics of all three. On the flight deck, there are different interactive styles. These are personality oriented and goal oriented. They can be plotted on a graph to determine the type of interactive behaviour you possess, such as 'Goal oriented, but not Person directed' G+P- (read as G plus P minus). You will look at the different types of leadership and learn which are preferable in a flight-deck environment. The factors affecting flight-deck interaction, such as age and experience, must also be understood. The way in which we communicate is an important consideration on a flight deck, as normally both pilots will be busy, minimizing body language. Therefore, we rely on verbal communication, especially with ATC.

Stress is an essential subject to study, as it can be found in many forms on and off the flight deck. You will need to understand the different types of stress and the general adaptation syndrome (GAS), which divides stress into three distinct phases. The ways in which we become stressed (stressors) must be appreciated, and not only life stressors, such as family death or unemployment, but also environmental stressors, such as heat and vibration. Different frequencies of vibration cause different stresses. You will need to be aware of the signs of stress – there will be health, behavioural, cognitive and subjective effects. The many ways of coping with stress are also studied.

Personality and Stress Sample Questions

1) What term is used to describe how a person reacts to demands placed upon them?
2) What are the easily observable indications of stress?
3) What are the effects on the body of vibrations in the 4–10Hz frequency range?
4) What are the three phases of the general adaptation syndrome?
5) How does Rasmussen classify the behaviour a pilot uses while carrying out a fire drill?

Flight-Deck Design

When developing an aircraft, flight-deck design is a very important factor. You will study anthropometry and will need an appreciation of the different types of measurement that can be taken. You will look at pilot seating – the eye datum point must be considered to ensure that the pilot has a good view at all times, and the seat must incorporate lumbar support to spread loads evenly over the pilot's spine. The electronic displays are studied, and you will need to know which type of information is best displayed digitally and which in analogue form, also the most easily understood form of altimeter. The positions of controls and switches are determined by a number of factors,

---

Flight-Deck Design Sample Questions

1) What is the most suitable type of display for indicating small rates of change?
2) Define anthropometry.
3) What is the most common checklist reading error?

---

such as frequency of use, sequence of use and importance; you must know these. Checklists are vital documents, sometimes being read during emergencies or under difficult conditions. Therefore, they must be designed so that they are easy to use. You will need an appreciation of how this is done. Automation has been a controversial topic in recent years, and you will need to be able to discuss its benefits and drawbacks.

Sleep and Fatigue

As the aviation industry works twenty-four hours a day, sleep and fatigue can be problematical. You must become familiar with the different types of fatigue and be aware of their symptoms. The body has rhythms, such as the circadian rhythm, which lasts around twenty-four hours. You will need to learn about zeitgebers, which are entraining agents that maintain this rhythm on a twenty-four hour cycle. When asleep, you will go through different stages, all of which must be known. You must also understand the function of sleep and the credit/debit system of sleep units. As an airline pilot, you are likely to cross time zones regularly. These crossings will affect the rhythms of your body, so you will need an appreciation of the effects and what can be done about them. There are disorders associated with sleep, including narcolepsy, apnoea and insomnia, and you must have a knowledge of all of them.

Sleep and Fatigue Sample Questions

1) In what direction of flight would it take longer to resynchronize a circadian rhythm?
2) During which period of sleep does rapid eye movement occur?
3) What is the maximum number of sleep credits that can be accumulated?
4) When is the body's core temperature normally at its lowest?

Learning

The process of learning can take place in many different ways, such as learning by insight, operant learning and learning by experience. You will need to know about these and the factors that may affect them. The learning process will be affected by Maslow's hierarchy of needs. This says that our needs must be fulfilled in a particular order. You should memorize Maslow's hierarchy of needs, as it often crops up in exam questions.

Learning Sample Questions

1) What are the highest and lowest needs in Maslow's hierarchy?
2) How is the quality of learning best promoted?
3) What are the two main tools for improving job satisfaction?

Flight Safety

Obviously, flight safety is the most important consideration for all airlines. Errors can be classified as design induced, operator induced, or faults and slips. You will need to know the definitions of these classifications and be able to put examples of errors into the correct categories. Rasmussen came up with a system for classifying errors, and it may prove useful to know the classifications in his system. The most important thing to learn from this section, however, is the SHEL model (Software, Hardware, Environment and Live ware), developed by Edwards in 1972. This is used as a basic aid to understanding human factors.

Flight Safety Sample Questions

1) According to Rasmussen's model, what type of errors occur in the skill-based control mode?
2) What does 'L' stand for in the SHEL model?
3) Selecting flaps rather than the undercarriage would be classified as what kind of error?

AVIATION LAW

A very large subject, Aviation Law simply requires you to commit information to memory. I found that the exam questions were such that if you did not know the answer, it was very difficult to work it out or make an educated guess. For me, the best way to study the subject was to read the relevant material and highlight or note all the numbers and tables. Then, when it came to revision, I simply needed to think of effective ways of remembering them. Another very effective way of learning the subject is simply to answer questions. There are many publications that contain thousands of Aviation Law questions, and much of my revision consisted of answering these. This makes any weak areas in your knowledge obvious, and you can take the necessary steps to improve them.

Since Aviation Law is so fact based, instead of discussing each aspect, I have listed the areas studied and provided sample questions. To go through everything required to be learned would require an extra book! The syllabus can be broken down into the following subject areas:

It is vital to have a good knowledge of aerodromes, since you will be making solo flights to them during the flying course.

- History
- Alerting Services
- Personnel Licensing
- Rules and Procedures of the Air
- Area Control Services
- Aerodrome Control Services
- Approach Control Services
- Radar
- Signals
- Flight Plans
- Aeronautical Information Service
- Holding Procedures
- Aerodromes
- Facilitation
- Altimeter Setting
- Security
- Interception
- Aircraft Registration
- Accident Investigation

OPERATIONAL PROCEDURES (OPS)

In many ways, OPS is very similar to Aviation Law. A substantial number of the items studied are identical or similar. I enjoyed much of the syllabus, as it is relevant to day-to-day operations, raising interesting questions and debates. The exam questions are of a similar style to those in Aviation Law,

Aviation Law Sample Questions

1) What is the required height of the registration markings on the fuselage and the vertical tail of heavier-than-air aircraft?
2) What is the meaning of the abbreviation PANS-RAC?
3) In an ILS approach, to what is obstacle clearance altitude referenced?
4) What is the speed limit for IFR flights inside controlled airspace classified as E, when flying below 10,000ft?
5) When should a pilot advise the appropriate air traffic unit of a deviation in TAS from the flight-plan value?
6) For how long is an instrument rating valid?
7) On what frequency should you try to get in contact with an intercepting aircraft?
8) What is the convention that deals with offences against penal law?
9) A flight information service shall be provided to aircraft to avoid collisions in which class of airspace?
10) What is the maximum speed adjustment that a pilot should be requested to make when under radar control, and established on intermediate and final approach?
11) Which International Civil Aviation Convention Annex covers personnel licensing?
12) To which convention do offences and certain acts on board an aircraft belong?
13) What is the absolute minimum to which radar separation may be reduced?
14) What is a descent or climb called in a holding pattern during an approach procedure?
15) In a standard holding pattern, which way are the turns made?
16) How may a braking action of 0.25 be described?
17) Using the ground–air visual code, what is the meaning of the symbol 'X'?
18) In an instrument departure procedure, what is the minimum obstacle clearance at the departure end of the runway?
19) What action should be taken if contact is lost with the runway on the downwind leg of a circling manoeuvre?
20) If a runway were closed for a year due to maintenance, where would this news be published?
21) An aircraft receives a series of red flashes from the control tower when in the airport's circuit. What does this signify?
22) What signal would a signalman use to ask the pilot to apply the parking brake?
23) What colour are taxiway edge lights?
24) What is the 'first freedom of the air'?
25) How many separate segments are there to an instrument approach procedure?

and the best way I found of learning the subject was to practise answering typical questions.

For success in the JAA exam, you will need a full understanding of everything in ICAO Annex 6, JAR-OPS, together with an appreciation of long-range navigation (i.e. crossing the Atlantic). It is very important to have a knowledge of the set-up of the various aviation authorities, and to be aware of who governs whom (e.g. ICAO, JAA and CAA). You will probably spend a lesson or two on this, which is a fundamental concept. You may find that some questions refer to JAA legislation rather than ICAO; this could affect the answer required.

For the long-range navigation section, it is necessary to review what you learned in the General Navigation syllabus about travelling great circles, grid navigation etc. Your study of gyros and compasses in the Instruments syllabus should also be revisited.

Operational Procedures Sample Questions

1) If smoke appears in the air conditioning, what should be your first action?
2) How many oxygen dispensing units must there be in the aircraft cabin if a public transport flight is to operate at flight level 390?
3) What kind of fires can be fought with an H_2O extinguisher?
4) At what altitude is there the greatest risk of a bird strike?
5) What is a Class A fire?
7) Who draws up the master minimum equipment list (MMEL)?
8) Where can the minimum equipment list (MEL) be found?
9) How would a runway covered in 4mm of water be described?
10) How many fire extinguishers should equip an aircraft with a maximum approved passenger seating configuration of 400?
11) During a night flight, what light would you see if an aircraft were approaching from the front right on a parallel track?
12) What transponder squawk code should be set in the event of a hijack?
13) A public address system is required in an aircraft if its maximum approved seating configuration is greater than…?
14) When does a life jacket become mandatory on an aircraft flying away from the shore?
15) If an engine pressure ratio (EPR) probe becomes covered in ice, what is likely to happen to its readings?
16) With what does ICAO Appendix 18 deal?
17) In which direction does astronomic precession cause a gyro to spin in the Northern Hemisphere?
18) Wake turbulence is most severe when an aircraft is in which of the following configurations?
   a) Slow
   b) Heavy
   c) Clean
   d) Flying with high thrust
19) For a pressurized aircraft, what altitude requires 30 per cent of the passengers to have an oxygen supply?
20) For a non-pressurized aircraft, at what altitude should all occupants of flight-deck seats on flight-deck duty have an oxygen supply?

FLIGHT PLANNING

In many ways, the Flight Planning syllabus is similar to the General Navigation syllabus. It is a lot more practical in the use of maps and charts, however, and you will be given more time in the exam to allow for this. Flight planning is necessary in the commercial world, as it allows an aircraft to carry the minimum amount of fuel for safe operation and maximum traffic load. For the exam, you will require the use of a *Jeppesen Airway Manual*, which will be issued to you for this purpose. You may be asked questions about any of the charts and information in the manual. You will make use of many of the techniques learned in the General Navigation syllabus, such as mathematical methods, and converting between nautical ground and nautical air miles. In the list of subject areas, you will see that point-of-no-return and point-of-equal-time techniques are included in the syllabus. Since these were discussed in Chapter 5, they will not be covered again in this chapter. Also, knowledge of traffic load is required, but this was part of the Mass and Balance syllabus (*see* Chapter 5), so it will not be discussed here. The Flight Planning syllabus can be broken down into the following subject areas:

- Planning a VFR Cross-Country Flight
- Fuel Planning
- Medium-Range Jet Transport (MRJT) Flight Planning
- Route Planning and Flight Plans
- Point of Equal Time (PET) and Point of No Return (PNR)
- Traffic Loads

Planning a VFR Cross-Country Flight
During your early single-engine flying, you will spend a lot of time planning cross-country flights under visual flight rules. To qualify for your Commercial Pilot's Licence, you will have to plan and fly a 300nm route with at least two en-route stops at different airports. It is important to select a route that is safe, so you must be able to read a VFR map and have an understanding of all the symbols used. Some exam questions may reproduce symbols for you to decode.

You will need to know the exact meaning of all the different types of airspace classification, from A to G. For an actual flight, you will fill in a personal flight plan, although you are not likely to be asked to do this in the exam. It is worth practising, however, as you may be asked questions about the methods used to fill in a personal flight plan, such as calculating an ETA from given information.

TIP
Make sure you have a good knowledge of the *Jeppesen Airway Manual*, as sometimes the answer to a question about a symbol will be in the symbols section at the front of the manual.

Planning a VFR Cross-Country Flight Sample Questions

1) Referring to chart ED-6, what is the track and distance between Friedrichschafen (EDNY) and Stuttgart (EDDS)?
2) Referring to chart E (HI) 4, what is the meaning of the symbol at Walda?
3) If the true course is 018°, the wind velocity is 350°/25kt and the TAS is 150kt, what are the wind correction angle and groundspeed?
4) Referring to chart ED-6, what is the frequency of the Rattenberg NDB?

Fuel Planning

An important part of the flight planning process is fuel planning. You will need to know all of the terminology that you were taught in Mass and Balance, and you will study extended-range operations (EROPS). You will probably refer to the CAA publication *CAP 697*, using the fuel graphs it contains to answer questions in the exam. There are separate single-engine piston (SEP) and multi-engine piston (MEP) graphs, which are quite self-explanatory, but you must practise using them until you can find answers quickly and accurately. To calculate fuel requirements, there is a graph for start-up, taxi and take-off to cruising altitude, together with tables to calculate fuel flow in the cruise. You can also calculate range and endurance using the graphs provided.

Fuel Planning Sample Questions

1) Refer to *CAP 697*, Figure 3.5. With forty-five minutes' reserve at 45 per cent power with economy cruise at 35,000ft, what is the endurance?
2) Refer to *CAP 697*, Figure 4.4. What is the holding fuel if an aircraft plans a straight and level hold at 210kt IAS for thirty minutes, at a pressure altitude of 3,000ft with a weight in the hold of 43,000kg?
3) What is the weight of 70 US gal of fuel with a specific gravity of 0.77?
4) What is the final reserve fuel for aircraft with turbine engines, and at what altitude is this assumed to occur?

Medium-Range Jet Transport Flight Planning

You will study a medium-range jet transport aircraft of similar size to the Boeing 737. The syllabus and *CAP 697* will guide you through planning for a flight on this aircraft. You must be able to calculate the optimum flight level, best endurance, range or speed, and fuel penalties for flying above or below the optimum altitude. These figures can be obtained using either simplified or detailed planning. The former method is much quicker than the latter, but not as accurate. You must be able to demonstrate both methods for the exam.

Medium-Range Jet Transport Flight Planning Sample Questions

1) Refer to *CAP 697*, Figure 4.7.2. What is the maximum diversion distance for an aircraft at M0.70/280kt approved with ninety minutes ETOPS and a mass of 48,000kg at the time of diversion?

2) Refer to *CAP 697*, Figure 4.5.1. What is the still-air distance and ground distance for an en-route climb at M0.74/280kt, given a brakes-release mass of 57,500kg, temperature ISA-10, a headwind component of 16kt and initially at flight level 280?

3) Refer to *CAP 697*, Figure 4.4. What is the fuel required for a thirty-minute hold in a racetrack pattern at a pressure altitude of 5,000ft and a mass of 47,000kg?

4) Refer to *CAP 697*, Figure 4.5.4. How much fuel will be consumed during a descent from 35,000ft to 5,000ft at a speed of M0.74/250kt?

In addition to fuel planning, there are abnormal operations that may need to be taken into account. These will also be found in *CAP 697*, which will specify the surplus fuel that must be burned off. The operations include single-engine flight, gear-down ferry flights, fuel tankering flights and extended-range operations. In each case, you will need to go to the relevant graph and follow the instructions supplied.

Route Planning and Flight Plans

Route planning for IFR flights will become an important factor when you start your instrument flying. You will need to know how to read airways, and have an appreciation of Standard Instrument Departures (SID) and Standard Terminal Arrival Routes (STAR). In the exam, you may be given a route and asked for the best airways to use, or you may be provided with a SID/STAR plate and asked questions about it. There is a lot of information on these charts, and the only way to be fluent in reading them quickly is to obtain plenty of practice. You will also look at approach plates, which provide all the information necessary to fly your aircraft from the end of the STAR and on to the runway. You will benefit if you have practised using these charts in the air before you take the exam, as this will give you an understanding of how the information is used. In addition, you may be asked to use some of the other charts from the *Jeppesen Airway Manual*, such as noise-abatement charts, airport plans and taxiing charts, so make sure you are familiar with them.

Prior to each instrument flight, you will have to submit a flight plan to give advance notice of the flight to all of the air traffic services that you will use or through whose airspace you will pass. You will need to know the deadline for submitting your flight plan, the information that is required, when you must inform ATC of deviations from the plan, what happens if any of the information changes and when you can use a repetitive flight plan for making regular identical flights. Blank flight plans will be freely available

> **TIP**
>
> In the *Jeppesen Airway Manual*, you will find a section on flight plans with instructions on how to use them. Consequently, you can refer to this if you do get stuck in the exam. Beware, however, as this will use up a lot of time.

Route Planning and Flight Plans Sample Questions

1) How long before start-up should a flight plan be submitted?
2) When can a repetitive flight plan be filed?
3) Refer to chart 20-3 for Paris in the *Jeppesen Airway Manual*. What is the distance of the departure route ABB 8A?
4) Using the same chart as in Question 3, what is the elevation of the aerodrome?
5) On a standard flight plan, what is considered as 'Standard Equipment'?

---

from your flying school's operations department, and it is worthwhile obtaining a few copies to familiarize yourself with them and practise completing them.

VFR AND IFR COMMUNICATIONS

For simplicity, I have combined VFR and IFR communications into one subject. I did this during my studies, as they are similar and relatively small. Another reason for doing this is that the two very short exams will occur one after the other. Furthermore, it seems to make one less subject to worry about!

If you have any choice, I would strongly advise that you take these exams after you have gained some flying experience. This is because many of the questions can be answered using simple common knowledge from your flying.

Because the communications exams are so much shorter than those of the other subjects, like Mass and Balance, they are very useful for boosting your overall average from the ATPL exams. Usually, there are only around twenty questions in each exam, and it is possible to get 100 per cent if you know the subjects really well.

First, you will need to know all of the definitions for the terminology used in radiotelephony. These are very specific, and the exam may try to catch you out on the detail. If you have not already learned the phonetic alphabet through flying, you will need to learn it now.

> **TIP**
>
> I used to practise the phonetic alphabet by trying to read car number plates out loud while driving.

Air Traffic Control will play a very important role in your flying; you will need to work well together.

You will need to know how time is expressed over the radio, and how all the call signs of the different air traffic services are expressed. A common exam question will ask you to list the importance of certain types of message, such as meteorological messages or flight safety messages, so it is essential that you learn these. Another common question will ask you for the parts of radio messages that must be read back to the controller. This is very important for your flying too; if your read-backs are correct during your flying tests, it will look very professional to the examiner.

As in Radio Navigation, you will study the accuracy of bearings given by ATC, so do not forget these once you have finished the former syllabus.

TIP

You can easily remember the items required in a position report by using the following mnemonic:

A – Aircraft identification
P – Position
T – Time
L – Level
N– Next position and time over it
E – Ensuing significant point

I used to remember this, as it sounds like ATPL Never Ends, but with the middle two letters of 'ATPL' mixed up.

> **TIP**
>
> If you are asked to enter a hold and do not know the holding procedure, ATC will pass you the information required in the following form:
>
> F – Fix
> L – Level
> I – Inbound track
> R – Right or left turns
> T – Time
>
> As you will notice, this spells FLIRT!

VFR and IFR Communications Sample Questions

1) What word is used by ATC to indicate the separation between portions of a message?
2) What does the abbreviation ATIS mean?
3) What is the exact meaning of the word 'Approved'?
4) What is the call sign for the aeronautical station that provides approach control (but no radar service)?
5) What status of message is one that concerns an aircraft being threatened by grave and imminent danger, requiring immediate assistance?
6) What is the amount of cloud cover when the term 'scattered' is used?
7) What phrase shall a pilot use to inform the control tower that they are ready for take-off?
8) What is the maximum distance that you might expect solid VHF contact over flat terrain at flight level 120?
9) If the pilot were unable to establish radio contact with an aeronautical station, what mode and code should they select on the transponder?
10) What does the phrase 'readability two' mean?

In some areas, position reporting is very important when there is no radar, so you will need to know what items make up a position report.

All radar phraseology must be known, including the meanings of the different transponder codes. You will also need an appreciation of what is provided by the different types of radar service, such as radar advisory service and radar information service. You must have an understanding of the difference between IFR and VFR flights in respect of radiotelephony.

You will need to know lots of information about meteorology, such as in-flight weather reports and when they should be given, special observations and the contents of an air report. The automated terminal information service (ATIS) is commonly used at most airfields, so you must have an appreciation of the information it provides and how often the information is updated.

It is almost certain that there will be an exam question on emergency messages, so you must be aware of the difference between a distress call and an urgency message. If you transmit one of these messages, you will need to know what information should be given. You should also be conversant with the speechless code. (There is no requirement to know Morse code, although this is very useful for identifying beacons.) Communications failures are not uncommon, so you will study the procedures to follow if your radios fail or, for some reason, you lose contact with any air traffic services.

CHAPTER 7
SINGLE-ENGINE
FLYING

Finally, with the exams over, you are allowed to step inside an aircraft! I remember the day well; it was a breath of fresh air after six months of full-time ground school, and it certainly was not an anti-climax. Enjoy your first lesson, because after that, the hard work will really begin. You will be due to go solo after about ten flights. If you have a PPL or some flying experience already, my advice would be to forget it and start this integrated training with a blank mind, as the way in which you will be taught is likely to be very different from any previous lessons. Each flying school has its own standards, and you need to learn them; if you simply stick to your previous school's standards, you may run into difficulties and run the risk of failing in-house tests.

It is very important to start learning about your aircraft as soon as you start flying. Since you will be flying solo in such a short time, would you really feel safe if you had no idea of how the aircraft worked or what was meant if one of the red lights came on? You will need to know the technical information anyway, as you are likely to be asked about it in the flying tests. If you start early, you will not have to cram it all in the night before a test.

A single-engine type such as this will be the first aircraft you actually fly on the course.

A Typical Single-Engine Flying Syllabus

Solo = You are the pilot in command of the aircraft; in tests, you may be con-
           sidered solo (under supervision) only if you pass.
Dual = You are flying the aircraft under instruction.
SPIC = Student pilot in command. This is used for instrument flights. Although
           you are the pilot commanding the aircraft, your instructor has overall
           authority, as you do not have an instrument rating and he must keep a
           lookout while you are using the instruments.

Lesson no.	Detail	Capacity
1	Effects of controls	Dual
2	Straight and level	Dual
3	Climbing, descending and turning	Dual
4	Climbing and descending 2	Dual
5	Stalling	Dual
6	Stalling	Dual
7	Stalling	Dual
8	Circuits	Dual
9	Circuits	Dual
10	Circuits	Dual
11	Circuits	Solo
12	Circuits	Dual
13	Circuits	Solo
14	Circuits	Dual
15	Circuits	Solo
16	General handling (GH)	Dual
17	Circuits	Solo
18	Circuits	Solo
19	Practised forced landings	Dual
20	Steep turns	Dual
21	Rejoins and circuits	Solo
22	Rejoins and circuits	Solo
23	General handling and VFR navigation	Dual
24	General handling	Solo
25	General handling	Solo
26	Basic instrument flying	Dual
27	General handling	Solo
28	VFR navigation	Dual
29	Basic instrument flying and GH	Dual
30	General handling	Solo
31	VFR navigation	Dual
32	VFR navigation	Solo
33	Basic instrument flying – tracking	Dual
34	General handling	Solo
35	VFR navigation	Solo
36	VFR navigation	Dual
37	VFR navigation	Solo
38	VFR navigation	Solo
39	Instrument flying – tracking, fixing	Dual
40	General handling	Solo
41	VFR navigation	Dual

Lesson no.	Detail	Capacity
42	VFR navigation	Dual
43	VFR navigation	Solo
44	VFR navigation	Solo
45 & 46	**Progress Test One**	Solo
47	VFR navigation	Solo
48	VFR navigation	Solo
49	Instrument flying	Dual
50	Instrument flying	SPIC
51	Instrument flying	SPIC
52	Instrument flying	SPIC
53	General handling	Solo
54	General handling	Solo
55	VFR navigation	Solo
56	VFR navigation	Solo
57	Instrument flying	SPIC
58	Instrument flying – holding	Dual
59	Instrument flying – holding	SPIC
60	Instrument flying – holding	SPIC
61	General handling	Solo
62	VFR navigation	Solo
63	Instrument flying	SPIC
64	IFR navigation	Dual
65	Instrument flying	SPIC
66	Instrument flying	SPIC
67	Instrument flying – land away	SPIC
68	Instrument flying – land away	SPIC
69	VFR navigation and GH	Solo
70	VFR navigation and GH	Solo
71	Instrument flying – land away	SPIC
72	Instrument flying – land away	SPIC
73	General handling	Solo
74	Instrument flying	SPIC
75	CPL cross-country qualifier	Solo
76	CPL cross-country qualifier	Solo
77	CPL cross-country qualifier	Solo
78	Instrument flying – land away	SPIC
79	Instrument flying – land away	SPIC
80	General handling	Solo
81	Instrument flying	SPIC
82	Revision for Progress Test 2	Dual
83	Revision for Progress Test 2	Solo
84	General handling	Solo
85	Instrument flying revision	SPIC
86	**Progress Test Two**	Solo
87	Instrument flying – land away	SPIC
88	Instrument flying – land away	SPIC
89	Instrument flying	SPIC
90	Night flying introduction	Dual
91	Night flying – navigation	Dual
92	Night flying – circuits	Dual
93	Night flying – circuits	Solo
94	Night flying – instruments	SPIC

You will need to know all about your aircraft from the outset.

The flying syllabus structure will differ from one training establishment to another; the amounts of hours allocated to single-engine and twin-engine flying may vary, as may the order of the lessons. I have given a typical structure that you could expect from an ATPL single-engine flying syllabus. Not all lessons constitute an hour. Also, depending on your progress, the weather and your instructor, the order of events is likely to be subject to change.

FLIGHT TIME

In total for the single-engine syllabus, you will probably amass around 118 hours of flying, including about sixty hours of navigation and forty-three hours of instrument flying. The total time will be broken down approximately as follows:

Dual flight time – 34.5hr
Solo flight time – 48.5hr
SPIC flight time – 35hr

During the single-engine stage of the course, you may find yourself using a synthetic flight training device, which is employed to introduce you to instrument flying. It will simulate your aircraft under instrument conditions, allowing you to practise instrument flying, such as tracking and holding. The device is for practice only, as it is cheaper than using a real aircraft. However, the time cannot be logged as time flown.

THE VALUE OF GROUNDWORK

You should receive a flying syllabus with all of the lessons broken down into components with targets. As a result, you will know what to expect and can do the necessary groundwork before flying. It is well worth spending plenty of time going through each flight in your head first, as this will prompt any questions you may have and will make life a lot easier in the air, saving you time and money. You could even use flight-simulator software on your computer to practise all of your flights, especially the instrument flying. This can also be employed for the basics, such as demonstrating the effects of flap or the effect on yaw when you increase or decrease power.

If your flight school has an aircraft with more than two seats, and if you have a good relationship with the other students on your course, it is very worthwhile coming to an arrangement whereby you sit in the back of each other's flights. This can be really beneficial. Although you will not be at the controls of the aircraft, you will see each lesson taught twice and see double the amount of mistakes being made (making mistakes is usually the best way to learn). Furthermore, you will spend lots of time familiarizing yourself with the local area, which is of great benefit when it comes to the tests.

After a long and tiring flight, it is very easy to go along to the debrief and not pay much attention to your instructor babbling on about how you did not use enough rudder or that you were too slow on final approach. However, the debrief is where you can do a lot of learning. The instructor will probably write notes on the flight, but it is important to make your own in a manner that makes sense to you. That way, nothing is left out. After the debrief with your instructor, sit somewhere quiet and debrief yourself. Run through what went well and what went badly, and replay the whole flight again in your mind, trying to think of any questions to ask before the next flight.

SOLO FLIGHT

The first solo is a very memorable occasion; it will make you extremely nervous and also excited. After a while, the nervousness will shrink and the excitement will grow. It is important not to let the quality of training lapse, however, just because you are enjoying yourself! Try not to approach a solo flight empty minded; before you get airborne, think of a plan of what you want to do and achieve during the flight. Have a list of things to do on your kneeboard, so that once you are positioned in the air, you can start running through them without having to think about what you would like to do next. After a few solos, you will know how long a stall or a practised forced landing takes, and you will be able to manage your time in the air efficiently. After a solo flight, it is worth

---

TIP
Using the same report form that your instructor employs, score yourself on solo flights and make notes on it. Before a test, read back through your own solo reports to remind yourself of the kinds of mistake that you have made in the past.

You will remember your first solo flight for your entire career.

giving yourself a debrief on everything that went well and why it went well. Consider the things that went badly too, work out why they went badly and decide what you need to practise next time. When flying solo, you will be given a crosswind limit – to fly, the wind must be below this value – but you may be able to have it increased by demonstrating to an instructor that you are capable of flying in such conditions. One day, you will probably find yourself stuck on the ground due to the crosswind, and it is very worthwhile dragging your instructor into the air for twenty minutes to gain the necessary experience. This will help you to get through the course quickly, as you will be able to fly on those windy days when otherwise you might have been grounded.

NAVIGATION

When you start navigating, there will be a large increase in the amount of equipment you have on your knee. You will not only have a kneeboard, but also a pencil, a map, a protractor, a rule and perhaps an OHP pen for drawing on the map. I spent a lot of time during navigation exercises with my head on the floor, desperately trying to find the pen that had fallen off my knee. After a few frustrating flights, I tied the pen to the kneeboard with a long piece of string – simple, yet it saved a huge amount of time and improved flight accuracy! Also, instead of carrying a large scaled rule, which will get in the way all of the time, try measuring other objects, such as your thumb, the edge of your protractor or your pencil, and use these instead. Normally, you do not need really accurate measurements in the air – when you are asked for a rough ETA for example – and this saves a lot of time.

PROGRESS TESTS

You can expect two or three tests in the single-engine flying part of the course. In my training, there were two progress tests. The first occurred after around forty-five hours of flying and was similar to a PPL skills test. No such licence was issued, however, as shortly after I took the CPL test.

You will spend a lot of time navigating around the skies on your own, so use anything you can to make it as easy as possible.

Progress Test One

A typical first progress test will cover most of the following items:

- Pre-flight documentation and weather
- Mass and balance, and performance calculations
- Aircraft inspection
- Engine starting
- Taxiing and aerodrome procedures
- Take-off
- Departure
- ATC liaison and airmanship
- Straight and level flight with speed changes
- Climbing and climbing turns
- Descending and descending turns
- Medium and steep turns
- Flight at low airspeed with and without flaps
- Stalling
- Flight plan and map reading
- Maintenance of an altitude, heading and speed
- Orientation, accuracy of ETA and log keeping
- Diversion
- Use of radio navigation aids and tracking them
- Basic instrument flying
- Flight management, fuel and systems checks
- Lost procedure
- Arrival procedure
- Landings (flapless, glide, precision touchdown, go-around)
- Simulated engine failure after take-off
- Simulated forced landing
- Emergencies
- Actions after flight

The test flight may be split into two sections, covering general handling and navigation. If you have a great flight in terms of handling, but get lost on the navigation exercise and cannot resolve the problem, you might pass the former and fail the latter, resulting in a partial pass. This means that you would need to take only the navigation part of the test again.

The second progress test is similar to the first, but with around an extra forty lessons behind you, a much more accurate and well-managed flight will be expected. You will be required to plan a longer diversion and be able to fly by referring only to the instruments. My second progress test was very similar to a CPL skills test in a single-engine aircraft.

Progress Test Two

In addition to the items covered in the first test, the second progress test will include:

- Tracking and positioning with use of a VOR or NDB, and identification of these facilities
- Level flight, controlling heading, altitude and speed with sole reference to instruments
- Climbing and descending turns with sole reference to instruments
- Recoveries from unusual attitudes with sole reference to a limited amount of instruments
- Flight accuracy
- Additional airmanship and flight management

How to Fail the Tests!

- Annoy your examiner before even starting the test by turning up late.
- Forget to keep a look-out for other aircraft. This is one of the most common reasons for failure. If you are not looking at anything for a reason, your head should be moving constantly in search of other aircraft, including behind you.
- Pay 'lip service'. Do not simply recite checklists without actually checking the items because you are too busy.
- Try out new things. The test is not the time for this; stick to what you know.
- Forget to take the cover off the pitot tube during your pre-flight inspection.
- Shut down the aircraft incorrectly. The test does not finish until you are out of the aircraft and the paperwork is complete.
- Think you have failed.

CHAPTER 8
TWIN-ENGINE
FLYING

It is at this stage of the course that you will probably feel the best. You will have completed all the ground school and be about to enjoy around three months of full-time flying, mostly on a twin-engine aircraft. This is what you have been waiting for! Depending on the school's syllabus, however, you are unlikely to step into a twin for some time yet. Initial training is done in an FNPT simulator (Flight, Navigation and Procedures Trainer). I still remember my first 'flight' in this; it was a fantastic experience. Unlike the synthetic flight training device used for the single-engine syllabus, this one may have some visual graphics, and it can be logged as simulator time.

The structure for the twin-engine syllabus is likely to be a short type rating so that you can sit the CPL skills test. Once you are a qualified commercial pilot, you will endure lots of time in the FNPT and some further aircraft time in preparation for the Instrument Rating (IR) test. Before sitting the IR skills test, however, you must pass a 170A test, which is intended to ensure that you are ready and capable of obtaining the rating. This is a CAA requirement. Flying a twin is great fun and a significant step up from a single. The basic flying principles are the same, but there are some major differences to learn, which will be discussed later.

The FNPT simulator.

A Typical Twin-Engine Flying Syllabus

Solo = You are the pilot in command of the aircraft; in tests, you may be considered solo (under supervision) only if you pass.

Dual = You are flying the aircraft under instruction.

SPIC = Student pilot in command. This is used for instrument flights. Although you are the pilot commanding the aircraft, your instructor has overall authority, as you do not have an instrument rating and he must keep a lookout while you are using the instruments.

Sim = Exercise carried out in the simulator.

Lesson no.	Detail	Capacity
1 (SIM)	Flight-deck familiarization	Sim
2 (SIM)	General handling	Sim
3 (SIM)	Abnormal procedures	Sim
4	General handling	Dual
5	General handling	Dual
6 (SIM)	Emergency procedures	Sim
7 (SIM)	Emergency procedures	Sim
8	Asymmetric flying	Dual
9	Asymmetric flying	Dual
10	Circuits	Dual
11 (SIM)	Basic instrument flying	Sim
12 (SIM)	Asymmetric instrument flying	Sim
13	Basic instrument flying	Dual
14 (SIM)	Emergency procedures	Sim
15	Navigation and handling	Dual
16 (SIM)	Instrument navigation and emergencies	Sim
17	Instrument navigation	SPIC
18	Commercial Pilot's Test Profile	Dual
19	**Commercial Pilot's Test**	Solo
20 (SIM)	Instrument flying – holding, tracking	Sim
21 (SIM)	Instrument flying – holding, tracking	Sim
22 (SIM)	Instrument flying – holding, tracking	Sim
23 (SIM)	Instrument flying – holding, tracking	Sim
24 (SIM)	Instrument flying – holding, tracking	Sim
25 (SIM)	Instrument flying – holding, tracking	Sim
26 (SIM)	Instrument flying – holding, approaches	Sim
27 (SIM)	Instrument flying – asymmetric approaches	Sim
28 (SIM)	Instrument flying – asymmetric approaches	Sim
29	Instrument flying	Dual
30 (SIM)	Instrument flying emergencies	Sim
31 (SIM)	Instrument landing system (ILS)	Sim
32 (SIM)	ILS and single-engine approaches	Sim
33	Route flight with ILS	Dual
34 (SIM)	Asymmetric ILS, SIDs, circling approaches	Sim
35 (SIM)	SIDs, emergencies, ILS, diversion	Sim

Lesson no.	Detail	Capacity
36 (SIM)	All instrument flying	Sim
37	All instrument flying	Dual
38	All instrument flying	SPIC
39 (SIM)	All instrument flying	Sim
40 (SIM)	All instrument flying	Sim
41	All instrument flying	SPIC
42	All instrument flying	SPIC
43 (SIM)	Simulated Instrument Rating Test	Sim
44	All instrument flying	SPIC
45	All instrument flying	SPIC
46	170A Flight Test	SPIC
47	**Instrument Rating Skills Test**	SPIC

FLIGHT TIME

In total for the twin-engine flying syllabus, you will probably amass around thirty-two hours of flying and forty hours in the simulator, including about fifteen hours of navigation and twenty-two hours of instrument flying. The total flight time will be broken down approximately as follows:

Dual flight time   – 15.5hr
Solo flight time (under supervision) – 1.5hr
SPIC flight time   – 15 hrs

PREPARATION AND PRACTICE

As with single-engine flying, preparation and practice is the key to success. For the visual flights before the commercial test, I found the best way to prepare was to run through the route in my head before taking the forecast wind into consideration, then to look for all the possible navigation problems along the way, such as high ground. It is very easy to prepare for instrument flights by using a computer-based flight simulator or other available programs. The only adverse effect could be caused by over-preparation, which could reduce your flexibility once airborne, so beware.

SINGLE VS. TWIN

Some of the main differences between flying a single and twin will be:

- The size – consider the extra wing and tail span when taxiing.
- The weight – you will have to give more consideration to inertia when changing speed, levelling off or turning, especially in the circuit.
- More instrumentation – there are double the amount of engine instruments, and generally twins are better equipped with navigation instruments too.

- The speed – everything happens a lot quicker, and any errors you make, such as those in heading, will escalate much more rapidly.
- Greater stability – pay lots of attention to trim – once the aircraft is nicely balanced, it will sit there without much need for correction.
- Better equipment – apart from more instrumentation, a twin will probably have better radios, perhaps heating and retractable landing gear.
- Two engines – you will not be required to carry out any more practised forced landings. You will have to learn how to fly on one engine, however, and make single-engine landings.
- Greater range – you will be able to fly to many more places because of a twin's higher speed.
- Operating costs – the cost of failing a flight test will be much more.
- A twin is more fun!

THE CPL AND INSTRUMENT RATING

There are two tests (excluding the 170A) during the twin-engine flying stage that you must pass. The CPL test is similar to the second progress test on the single-engine aircraft, but instead of the simulated forced landing section, it deals with the asymmetric approach. The Instrument Rating test will be the final flying test of the ATPL course and will include some en-route flying, approaches and emergencies. There are a couple of simple formulas that might help you during the instrument flying training (*see* TIPS).

CPL Skills Test
The skills test for your Commercial Pilot's Licence covers the following items:

- Pre-flight documentation and weather
- Mass and balance, and performance calculations
- Aircraft inspection

TIPS

To calculate the speed you are travelling per minute, simply divide your groundspeed by 60. For example, 150 / 60 = 2.5nm/min. Now you can quickly work out an ETA.

The examiner could ask you to divert anywhere, even to a strange airport. Print off the details for each airport, fold them up and organize them neatly with clearly marked labels. That way, if you do suddenly have to go to a strange airport, you can pull out the relevant arrival details easily.

To calculate the rate of descent required on an ILS glide path, simply divide your groundspeed by 2 and add a 0. For example, 120/2 = 60; 60 + 0 = 600ft/min.

For the tests, you may be asked to give a take-off and a passenger brief. To make sure you do not miss anything, have one prepared on your kneeboard and use blank spaces for the variables, such as runway in use.

Enjoy your flights and take a camera on some of them!

- Engine starting
- Taxiing and aerodrome procedures
- Take-off
- Departure
- Altimeter setting
- ATC liaison and airmanship
- Straight and level flight with speed changes
- Climbing and climbing turns
- Descending and descending turns
- Medium and steep turns
- Flight at low airspeed with and without flaps
- Flight at critically high airspeed, including recognition and recovery from a spiral dive
- Stalling
- Flight plan and map reading
- Maintenance of an altitude, heading and speed
- Orientation, accuracy of ETA and log keeping
- Diversion
- Engine failure after take-off
- Asymmetric flight (go-around, approach and landing)
- Flight management, fuel and systems checks
- Lost procedure
- Arrival procedure
- Landings (flapless, glide, precision touchdown, go-around)
- Simulated engine failure after take-off
- Flight with reference solely to instruments
- Recoveries from unusual attitudes with reference solely to some of the instruments
- Tracking and position fixing using a correctly identified beacon
- Emergencies
- Actions after flight

As with other tests, navigation and handling are dealt with separately, so it is possible to pass one and not the other, and be granted a partial pass. Once you have passed the complete test and have received your licence, you will be qualified to fly for reward or money.

The Instrument Rating Test

The final test that you will have to pass to walk away from the flying school with a frozen ATPL is for your Instrument Rating. Usually, this does not last as long as the other tests, and it has the advantage that you can fly in the type of adverse weather conditions that would prevent a CPL skills test. The Instrument Rating test is the only test that must be taken with a representative from the CAA. It will be divided into six sections, and if you

Your pre-flight walk-around must be thorough. You could fail the test before even getting into the aircraft if you forget to check something properly.

fail any of them, you will receive a partial pass. The sections are:

1. Departure
2. General handling
3. En-route
4. Precision approach
5. Non-precision approach
6. Simulated asymmetric flight

The Instrument Rating test will be marked on the following aspects:

- Pre-flight documentation and weather
- Preparation of ATC flight plan and an IFR log
- Mass and balance, and performance calculations
- Aircraft inspection
- Engine starting
- Taxiing and aerodrome procedures
- Take-off
- Transition to instrument flight
- Instrument departure procedure
- ATC compliance

- Control of the aircraft with reference solely to instruments
- Climbing and descending turns
- Recoveries from unusual attitudes
- Stalling
- Limited-instrument-panel straight and level flight and unusual-attitude recoveries
- Tracking, including interception
- Use of radio aids
- Timing and revision of ETAs
- Monitoring of flight progress, flight log, fuel and systems
- Ice protection procedures
- Arrival procedures
- Approach and landing brief
- Holding procedure
- Approach timing, altitude, speed and heading control
- Go-around and missed-approach procedure
- Simulated engine failure after take-off
- Asymmetric approach and landing

All being well, you will fly through this test with no problems. All the hard work will have paid off and you can start applying for that dream job at last!

How to Fail the Tests!

- Identify a failed engine incorrectly. Rely on the feel of the controls, not the engine gauges.
- Not noticing the examiner removing circuit breakers, such as the stall warning device, and consequently you wait for the stall warning, which never occurs, resulting in a stall. Keep a lookout for mischievous examiners!
- Admit that you are lost on your CPL navigation exercise. Keep flying on your calculated heading and time, and hope that a recognizable feature appears; it can save you the test.
- Fly an unstable ILS approach. This is one of the commonest ways of failing the Instrument Rating; fly the attitude, not the needles.
- Try to write down a missed-approach procedure in the middle of flying an approach, as you will lose flying accuracy. Instead, roll up your sleeve corresponding to the direction in which you were asked to turn and use another prop for the heading, such as an unused omni bearing selector (OBS) instrument.
- Forget to change the altimeter pressure setting for the approach and landing. Devise some method of remembering to alter the setting from the standard pressure setting (1013hPa) used in the cruise. (*See also* Chapter 7.)

CHAPTER 9
MULTI-CREW
CO-OPERATION
COURSE

The Multi-Crew Co-operation (MCC) course will provide the foundations you need to work as a crew member, rather than as a single pilot, which would have been the case up to this point in your training. Once you are working for an airline, you should never have to fly as a single pilot again. This course will demonstrate the advantages and problems of being a crew member, and teach you the skills required to make a good multi-crew pilot. Depending on where you decide to train, you may also learn the main differences between flying a jet and flying a light aircraft. There will be a lot to think about!

At the end of the MCC course, you should have the skills to work in a flight-deck team, with the ability to communicate well, share and prioritize tasks, use checklists, and supervise and monitor other crew members. A good MCC course will not only teach you about the flight-deck team, but also make you aware of the need to consider other personnel, such as ground crews, dispatchers, company operations staff and the cabin crew. The course is likely to consist of around a week of ground school, where you will look at what makes a good or bad crew, followed by around sixteen hours of flying in a crew environment. You will probably delve deeper into many of the theories studied in the Human Performance and Limitations syllabus (*see* Chapter 6), such as the SHEL model, different types of personality and behaviour, authority and cockpit gradients, and even pilot incapacitation. Previous aircraft incidents may be used as examples of both poor and good MCC, so expect to see some footage of previous disasters.

During the flying phase, you will make a number of separate flights, sharing the command equally with your crew member. Initially, the flights will cover familiarization, then you will move on to procedural approaches, emergencies and route exercises.

THE PAPER BOMBER

I found it very useful to work with my crew member out of the simulator, practising all of the flights in front of a paper representation of the flight deck, sometimes referred to as a 'paper bomber'. This saved a lot of simulator time, as we had already learned the procedures required prior to each simulator session. As a result, the lessons went smoothly and quickly, allowing us to move on to new aspects beyond the normal scope of the course.

The course cannot be failed, and there is no requirement to learn how to fly a jet, or to memorize lots of checklists. It is a great opportunity to learn something useful, however, and it will prove very valuable when carrying out a simulator assessment during the selection process for an airline. If you put lots of effort into this course, you will achieve great results, which could make the difference between passing or failing an airline selection.

TIPS

- Practise, Practise, Practise, Practise! (Use the paper bomber.)
- After a debrief with your simulator instructor, hold your own crew debrief.
- Fly 'raw data' (no use of flight director or autopilot) where possible. It is great practice for a simulator assessment with an airline.
- Try to memorize examples of good and/or bad MCC that you experience during the course. You can use these in answers to interview questions.

Chapter 10
Finding a Job

Having successfully completed the ATPL course, you can set off with your licences tightly clutched in one hand and your CV in the other. The final task of gaining employment is ahead of you. The ATPL course was incredibly hard work, but the hardest part of all is about to start.

FINDING VACANCIES

During the ATPL course, from the very beginning, try to keep up to date with airline current affairs, noting which companies are ordering or receiving aircraft and when. This will give you a good idea of the airlines that are likely to need more pilots and which may be expanding or contracting.

The best way of finding job vacancies may be through your flying school. They do talk to airlines in search of new business, and they are likely to know which companies are recruiting or not recruiting. Therefore, it is very important to maintain a good relationship with the school, as this is the time that you will really need its help! Some training establishments operate recommendation schemes with airlines, and depending on how you performed throughout the course, your school may suggest you for an interview if it believes you are suitable for a particular airline.

Vacancies are often advertised in aviation magazines, although usually these are for type rated pilots. If an airline is advertising for such aircrew, the company must be short staffed, so it may be worth applying anyway, in the hope that it will consider you if it cannot find the rated pilots it needs. The Internet is another good source of vacancies. They can be found on aviation job sites, or you can go directly to the recruitment pages of airline websites. Many airlines have online application forms or a means of entering your details to register your interest in the company. Directories are obtainable containing details of all the world's airlines; a copy of this list will prove very useful in Internet searches.

BALPA holds a pilot recruitment conference every year, during which many airlines will give presentations on their current and future pilot requirements. Some excellent information can be obtained, not only about vacancies, but also about the companies themselves, which you can use during interviews. Take lots of copies of your CV and have some business cards printed, as you will have the opportunity to meet many chief pilots and recruitment managers, who may well be interested in you. Dress smartly!

To attend the conference, you will need to join BALPA; it offers a discounted rate for student pilots. Purchase a ticket for the conference well in advance, ideally during your ATPL training.

Network! Your fellow flying school students will be searching for vacancies just as vigorously as you, so keep in touch and share information.

YOUR CV

Although most airlines employ online application forms and do not ask for separate CVs, there will be occasions when a CV is very important. Small airlines that do not have websites usually require a CV for the initial screening process. A company to which you have been recommended by your flying school may ask for a CV before inviting you to an interview, so that it can learn a little about you. A CV is a very handy document to carry at pilot recruitment conferences and the like. There are many different ways of creating a CV, and as time passes, the requirements change. However, I have provided some suggestions for your to consider:

- Keep it personal. Try assembling your own CV before looking at any others, so that your CV is personal. Look at other CVs later to make sure you have not missed out anything important.
- Keep it simple. Consider restricting your CV to one side of an A4 sheet. It should not be a detailed account of your life, just a brief snippet to interest a prospective employer in contacting you for more.
- Consider a photo. Whether or not you include a photo is a personal choice, but I believe it is worth adding a small head-and-shoulders photo of you wearing your uniform. This allows a potential employer to put a face to your name before meeting you.
- Put your flying experience somewhere near the top of the CV. Not only will the employer want to look at this first, but it will be most important to you after all, and you will want to show that you are proud of it. If you achieved good results, do not be modest, state them (e.g. 'All flight tests passed on first attempt' or 'Ground school average – 99 per cent'). If your results were not as good as you had hoped, do not lie, just exclude the details!
- Include a brief academic background.
- Add a brief background of other achievements and hobbies. It does not matter how minor they are. Try to include lots of teamwork.
- Think carefully about including such details as being a smoker, being married or holding a clean driving licence. Are these really relevant to your application at this stage?

MAKE YOURSELF KNOWN

Talk to people! During your time at the flying school, airline representatives may visit occasionally. If you get the chance, have a chat with them, as you never know when you might bump into them again. You could send them a letter a few weeks later to let them know of your progress, then send another when you qualify.

Do not be frightened to try to get hold of the person in charge! Most people would refrain from contacting the chief pilot or even the managing director, but if you do, it might just make a difference. If possible, visit the person's office to meet them face to face; if you send a letter, it might never even make it into their hands.

INTERVIEW TIPS

Interview styles are likely to differ from one company to another. Some may be long and formal, while others may take the form of a short, informal chat. You should prepare carefully for an interview, bearing in mind the following points:

Sample Interview Questions

Here are a few of the more challenging interview questions that I have encountered from a variety of companies:

1) Give an example of a bad decision that you have made.
2) Give an example of an occasion when you demonstrated bad leadership.
3) Describe a leadership situation where other group members disagreed with your decision.
4) Give an example of a situation you have been in where teamwork has broken down. What did you learn?
5) What sort of communicator are you?
6) Would you deviate from standard operating procedures?
7) Would you lie for the company?
8) What causes you stress? How do you cope? Do you have any side-effects?
9) Have you experienced different cultures and what did you learn?
10) Do you take risks?
11) Please give an example where you have had to deal with racial diversity as the leader of a small team. Also, explain how you persuaded the other team members to see your point of view.
12) (Question to an ex-University Air Squadron member.) If you enjoy flying so much, why did you not join the RAF?
13) Would you cross a picket line?
14) Define customer service. Which customers should we value most, economy or business passengers?
15) How would you question a captain's judgement?
16) Who else have you applied to and why?

As you can see, many of the questions require a negative answer. However, do not leave it at that. Give the negative answer, but then quickly go on to explain what you learned from the experience and what you could have done better, or how you have done better since. This allows you to finish on a positive note.

- Prepare in advance and practise! Ask friends to give you practice interviews.
- Make sure you have lots of life experiences to talk about, such as occasions when you have worked in teams that have gone well or bad, or when you have had to resist peer pressure. If you think of plenty of life experiences before the interview, you will be surprised at how many are relevant to the questions asked.
- Take along your licences, medical certificate, national insurance number, passport, logbook and a few copies of your CV.
- Wear a good, clean, conservative suit.
- Read up on interview techniques. There are many books on this subject, and they do give valuable advice on important considerations, such as first impressions and body language.
- When your interviewers introduce themselves, try to memorize their names so that you can use them during the interview or at the end.
- Do not let one or two hard questions ruin your interview. Simply ask politely if you can return to the subject later. If the interviewer does not forget about it in the meantime, you may be able to think of an answer as the interview progresses.

CAN'T GET A JOB?

Finding yourself in a position where you are unable to get that dream job and your loan repayments are fast approaching will be very worrying, but the situation is one that you would have considered before embarking on the course. There may be ways around the difficulty; you need to be a little imaginative and determined not to give up.

The first solution that will become apparent is to become a flying instructor. This may not be the flying job you had in mind, but it is a job for which you will be paid to fly. Instructing can be rewarding, although the pay is not very good initially, and you may find it hard to make loan repayments. Consequently, an extra part-time job may be required. As an instructor, you will be able to maintain your hours, keep your licence current and, most importantly, remain 'in the loop'. You will stay in contact with the aviation world and be able to continue networking.

Another option is to seek non-flying employment within an airline, perhaps as a dispatcher. Such jobs often offer lots of overtime, which you can use to fund a few hours flying here and there. Keep your licence current, show an interest in the airline, and work hard, and just maybe when the company requires pilots, your CV will be on the top of the pile.

Look for scholarships. In the past, GAPAN has offered scholarships for jet orientation courses (JOC) and instructors' ratings, both of which could help your airline career take off. If a scholarship is not available, you may be able to complete a JOC at your own expense, although you will have to return to your bank and request a little more money. Before choosing a JOC training provider, ask if it will be able to recommend you to any airlines, and investigate the amount of success it has had in finding employment for JOC graduates.

Don't Give Up!

Finally, do not give up in the search for your dream job. Those who have done so are struggling to pay off their loans from an office desk, watching the airliners fly overhead and are dreaming still!

Chapter 11
Life on a Flying
School Campus

LIVING AWAY

Throughout my training, I found that there were advantages and disadvantages to living away from home. The studying environment where I trained was excellent, and being away from home ensured that I put 100 per cent of my concentration into studying for the ground-school exams and preparing for the flying. At times, however, living away became frustrating. I missed my family and friends and a social lifestyle, and it became very boring, claustrophobic and lonely. That said, the residential course did allow me to achieve my full potential, giving me the best chance of succeeding in the course.

Depending on where the training takes place, the climate can have a significant effect. Good sunny weather does mean that the flying progresses very quickly. I do believe, however, that flying in bad weather is extremely important, as this will give you the experience and confidence you will need when flying to less-clement destinations during your airline career. Good weather will also make your efforts to sit down and study much more difficult, especially if there is an inviting swimming pool outside your door!

Living away normally means that you will have the opportunity to meet new people and make some great new friends. I found that being with people who were going through exactly the same experiences really did help. Different people have different strengths and weaknesses, and you will be able to work as a team to help each other through the course. If there are any personality clashes, however, they may cause some strain within the course and could make the experience difficult. As a trainee airline pilot, though, it is important that you are a good 'people' person and have the ability to deal with personality clashes, as you may have to spend many hours on the flight deck with similar people.

Another benefit of living away is that you get to see somewhere new, whether it is abroad or at home. If the former, you may be able to learn a new language at the same time, which will make you even more attractive to airlines at home, and enable you to apply to some overseas airlines as well. Learning a new language takes time and dedication, however, and you must not allow it to have a detrimental effect on your performance in the ATPL syllabus. Being abroad, you will also experience another culture, where the food, religion, dress code, working hours, daylight hours and general way of life may all be very different.

A major disadvantage of living away from home is that being away from friends, family, your children or loved ones for such a long period of time may get you down and lower your morale. This can be problematic, especially at times of high workload and stress, such as when taking exams. Living on a campus for well over a year, you will probably feel the need to get away quite often. When abroad, however, this can become difficult or expensive if the nearest town is a long distance away. Also, the language barrier in foreign countries may cause some problems when trying to go out to relax and forget about the stresses of the course, or simply for general day-to-day activities, such as shopping. The cost of visiting home at Christmas, Easter and other special occasions can push up your expenses, so remember to budget for this if appropriate.

FACILITIES

The prime advantage of living on an all-inclusive campus when training for your ATPL is that you can put all of your time and effort into studying and flying. Daily chores, such as cleaning your room and cooking, need not be considered. Everything is provided, so you can maximize your study time.

Living on campus abroad definitely has its advantages!

I found it useful to take regular exercise, whether it was going for a run or playing football. I felt that this kept my mind active. You may find that the campus offers such facilities as a gym, a swimming pool, tennis courts or even a table-tennis table, all of which are great benefits.

It would almost be possible to spend the whole period of the course on an all-inclusive campus, and never have the need to leave. Being in the same place for long periods of time may become frustrating, however, and I would suggest obtaining or borrowing transport so that you can escape and enjoy yourself from time to time!

MEETING NEW PEOPLE

On the first day, you will meet the students with whom you will be about to embark on a long and difficult course. At that point, it will seem strange to think that those people will become your very good friends, and that you may come to rely on each other and work as a great team. Whether for studying ground school, flying or personal issues, there will be strengths and weaknesses within the group, and it will really help if you can support each other. During my training, I was amazed at the varying backgrounds, nationalities and ages of those training with me.

At times, however, it may feel a little claustrophobic within the group. You will be spending every day together training, not to mention meal times and evenings. You will even socialize together, and will probably sleep next door to each other! I would advise that occasionally you make the time to get away and take a break from your course mates. That way, you will enjoy their company much more. Depending on the individuals within your group, you may notice a tendency for competitiveness to develop. I watched this occur in most courses and would strongly advise that you do not get involved, as it makes everyone's life a lot more difficult and stressful.

THE ATMOSPHERE

Living life on a small campus with perhaps hundreds of similar people, all with a common goal, on a very expensive course and with a competitive employment market is asking for difficulties! On the whole, I enjoyed the lifestyle and made some great friends, but news does travel very fast in these conditions. Nothing remains a secret for long, and everybody talks about everybody else. For example, when I passed one of my flying tests, half the people on the campus seemed to know that I had passed before even I knew!

A great benefit of being in such an atmosphere, however, is that on special occasions, such as Christmas, parties, Halloween and summer barbecues, everyone is usually interested in taking the time to relax and enjoy themselves, so they are great fun!

CHAPTER 12
PRACTICALITIES

Here, I have listed a few of the practicalities of taking an integrated ATPL course. They may not be relevant to all courses, but they may trigger some ideas before you start.

- Take an alarm clock with you.
- Have some good-quality business cards printed, send them out with CVs and take them wherever you go; you never know when you may meet someone useful. Include a small picture if possible so that people will remember your face.
- If possible, take a laptop on the course with you. It will be great for writing applications and your CV, ensuring that it is ready for the day you gain your CPL. You can also use it with the ground-school revision software that is available from aviation stores.
- Keep your own electronic logbook on a spreadsheet package. This will be very useful indeed when you come to fill in your licence application forms or airline application forms that ask for unusual breakdowns of your flying hours.
- Keep a record of all the flights that are cancelled and the reasons for cancellation. If the end of the course is approaching and you are well behind schedule, the flying school may say that this is your problem and may charge you for extra accommodation. If you have a good record of the reasons you are behind (such as aircraft technical problems) and they were beyond your control, the school may have to reconsider its charges.
- Buy a cheap digital watch to attach to your kneeboard; they are excellent for timing navigation legs.
- Make sure you have a very good pair of sunglasses. You will be spending a lot of time above the clouds at altitude, and in this career, you need to look after your eyes.
- Since you are about to embark on around 200 hours of flying, it will be worth spending a little money on a good, comfy headset.
- Take a passport at all times when flying, even if you are going nowhere near another country. If the weather changes and you have to divert, it might come in handy.
- If you are not happy with the instructor you have been given, you have the right to complain and ask for another. Make sure it really is a serious

problem, however, as the request will be noted in your training file. As a pilot, you must be able to get on with fellow crew members. Unfortunately, some people may come to the conclusion that your request for a change in instructor means that you are unable to do this.

- Keep a rough logbook throughout your flying and fill in a neat version once all your hours have been finalized. This saves carrying your logbook around everywhere, which will ruin it, and prevents all the mistakes being seen; there will be lots! When attending an interview, the company will look at your logbook. If it is neat, clear and professional looking, with no mistakes, it will give you a great start.

CHAPTER 13
STUDY METHODS

The first few weeks of ground school will cover the basic principles of all the subjects that will lay the foundations for the rest of the course. Depending on where you train, however, the learning curve is likely to be very steep. At the beginning, the workload will not be too great, so it is well worth enjoying yourself and making the most of the benefits of living on a campus. If you are training abroad, you should grasp the opportunity to take in the local culture, as very soon you will not have the time to do so.

SUMMARIZE YOUR WORK

From the outset of ground school, I made a big effort to write a summary of each lesson (I had six one-hour lessons per day). This could take around two hours every evening, and having a second look at each lesson helped them to sink in. To save time in the evenings, I would use the breaks between lessons or the lunchtime to write my summaries. That way, I managed to have most of the evening time free; it just meant working extra hard during the day. At the weekends, I would allocate half a day to read through the previous week's summaries and half a day to test myself with some sample exam questions on the relevant topics. The remaining day was work-free for relaxation.

As the ATPL exams approached (around four weeks beforehand), I started to summarize my summaries. The exam pressure really begins to build at this point, and any evenings and weekend days originally allocated as free time will probably disappear. Each summary created a few pages of notes that listed everything I needed to know for each exam. There is little point in writing down anything with which you are extremely confident or have committed to memory. By now, it is worthwhile starting to practise answering exam-style questions. There are thousands of them available, and the more you do, the greater the chance of encountering some of them in the real exams.

STRUCTURED REVISION

Depending on your training school, you may be given a week or so free of lessons so that you have plenty of time to revise. During this time, it is well worth developing a structured timetable, so that you do not spend too much time on

PHASE 2

	Am	Pm	Eve
Mon 28 Mar	Timetable	Timetable	3 Ch's | OPS
Tuesday	F	F	ops
Wednesday	Time table	Timetable	OPS
Thursday	F	F	inst
Friday	Time table	Time table	HPL | Inst
Saturday	~~OPS~~ perf ch 11 Q's	Perf	HPL
Sunday	LAW	LAW	LAW
Mon 04 April	G/S	G/S	F.P
Tuesday	FLY	FLY	fly (PT)
Wednesday	FLY	FLY	off
Thursday	F.P	F.P	Perf
Friday	G/S	G/S	JAA Perf / LAW (NOS)
Saturday	INST (GYROS) + FB	LAW	LAW FB
Sunday	OPS	OPS	~~INST~~ ops
Mon 11 April	Comms	Comms	HPL
Tuesday	Perf	HPL	~~FP~~ LAW
Wednesday	F.P	F.P Practice	OPS
Thursday	INST	INST	PERF
Friday	~~PERF~~ INST	~~PERF~~ INST	~~OPS~~ INST
Saturday	perf	law	HPL
Sunday	F.P	OPS	INST
INST, OPS, FP — **Mon 18 April**	MOCKS		?
Tuesday	Comms / HPL	Perf	LAW
Law, HP, Perf, Comms — **Wednesday**	MOCKS		—
Thursday	—	— / INST	INST
Friday	INST	INST	LAW
Saturday	PERF	PERF	OPS
Sunday	HPL	HPL	F.P
Mon 25 April	LAW	HPL	F.P
Tuesday	PERF	INST	OPS
Wednesday	HPL	HPL	LAW
Thursday	INST	LAW/OPS	HPL
Friday	OPS	PERF	Comms
Saturday	HPL	INST	Law
Sunday	LAW	INST ~~LAW~~ / HPL	HPL
Mon 02 May	PERF	OPS / FP / INST →	INST
Tuesday	PERF	PERF (PERF)	INST / OPS / FP
Wednesday	(INST) (OPS)	(F PLANNING)	Comms
Thursday	HPL HPL	Comms	LAW LAW
Friday	(AIR LAW) (HPL)	(COMMS)	HOME!
Saturday			
Sunday			

} mocks

Perf = 3.5
Law = 3.5
ops = 2.5
inst = 3.5
F.P = 1
HPL = 4
Comms = 2

Notes

3 *Perf - Go through graphs, & notes, do FB.

3 *Law - Learn numbers & do FB!

1.5 Ops - Learn Oxygen, wake turb, circling heights, ILS minima, emergency equip + FB

3.5 *Inst - Go over AF & rest, + FB

1 FP - Practise Q's!

3 HPL - Run through notes & do FB

VFR -

IFR -

one subject to the detriment of another. I used to split the day into three parts – morning, afternoon and evening – and allocate each to a subject.

It is a matter of personal choice, but I felt most confident about sitting an exam if I knew that I had covered everything possible for each subject. This meant that I had to read every manual again from start to finish, noting anything of which I was unsure. Although this is time consuming, it does ensure that you do not miss anything, and reading everything again is not a bad way of revising. As I was revising, if I found anything, such as a mnemonic, that helped me remember something, or if there was something that was hard to memorize, I would write it in a small notebook, which had a section for each exam. Just before walking into the exam room, I would flick through these notes and, before starting the exam, jot them down on a piece of paper. It really did help.

As each exam approached, I found myself preferring to spend my time doing 'feedback' (sample exam questions). There is an art to answering multiple-choice questions, and I believe that practising helps. As you work through the sample questions, try to answer them under exam conditions so that you become used to the time pressure, and also so that you can obtain a score. If you keep the scores on record, a few days before the exam, you can check them to discover the subjects that need more work. In addition, keep a record of the questions that you answered incorrectly (or only got right because you guessed). Write out each question and answer in full to create a 'wrong question sheet' for each subject. The next time you are about to sit a paper for that subject, have a look over this sheet – your mark should improve drastically from the time before!

Chapter 14
Other Routes to the Right-Hand Seat

As discussed previously, in addition to the integrated course, you can train for an ATPL through a modular course. This means taking each part of the qualification separately over a longer period of time, but at a lower cost. This route also allows you to earn the money needed before each part. The modular method has proved successful for many years, and many airlines will consider modular trained students.

The modular syllabus where I trained for the CPL and Instrument Rating was quite different from the integrated syllabus. In addition, modular courses will vary considerably from one school to another. Furthermore, there is no reason why the training cannot be adjusted to suit your needs if you already have some flying experience or hold another flying qualification.

BECOME AN INSTRUCTOR

If you are struggling to find any flying employment, becoming a flying instructor is an option that will enable you to gain flying hours and experience while earning some money (although not a lot). You will have to take a flying instructor's course, the minimum requirements for which are as follows:

- A valid aeroplane licence, including a single-engine class or type rating.
- The knowledge requirements of a Commercial Pilot's Licence.
- 200 hours flying time on aeroplanes (150 hours of which must be as pilot in command if you only hold a PPL, or 100 hours if you hold a CPL).
- Pass a pre-entry flight test with an examiner within six months of the start of the course.
- Thirty hours' flying on a single-engine piston aeroplane (five hours of which must be in the six months preceding the pre-entry flight test).
- Ten hours of instrument flight instruction (of which a maximum of five may be instrument instruction on a simulator).

- Twenty hours of cross-country flight time as pilot in command, and a cross-country flight of at least 300nm with two stops at different airports from that of the departure.

Opinions differ about using instructing as a method of getting into an airline. Some airlines prefer not to take ex-flying instructors, arguing that the hours they have amassed are not 'quality' hours. Others, however, appear to like ex-flying instructors. So it would seem to depend on whether or not you fit an airline's profile. Flying instructors often say that theirs is a very rewarding job; watching someone you have trained going solo is supposed to be very satisfying. It is a means of doing the job you have dreamed of. So there are advantages and disadvantages to this route, but with a little luck and determination, eventually it could put you into an airliner's right-hand seat.

TRY THE MILITARY

If you really love flying, there are many excellent opportunities in the military. If you particularly want to fly for an airline, bear in mind that many airline pilots are ex-military pilots. This is an excellent route on to the airliner's flight deck, as the training is second to none. You will have to accept that becoming an airline pilot will be your second career, however, as first you must pursue a career in the military, which will require a long commitment. Becoming a military pilot is not an easy task. Only the best are taken on, and there is an exhaustive selection programme of aptitude tests, interviews, group exercises and fitness tests.

The general requirements for application for training as a military pilot are:

- Five GCSEs/SCEs and two A levels, or three Highers or equivalent. GCSEs/SCEs at Grade C/3 minimum to include English Language and Mathematics
- Nationality: British citizen since birth, or holder of dual British/other nationality

Having been trained as a military pilot, not only will you have excellent flying skills, but also you will be in a good position for a future airline career. Nothing is guaranteed, however, since every airline will have its own particular pilot profile; if you do not meet it, the company will not spend money on training you on commercial aircraft.

Military Pilot Minimum Service Periods

RAF Pilot	– 12 Years
Army Pilot	– 7 Years
Royal Navy Pilot	– return of service of 3–5 years, depending on branch

CHAPTER 15
AFTER THE JOB OFFER

After I had completed a selection process for an airline, including aptitude tests and interviews, it was not long before I was told that I had been successful and was offered a jet orientation course with the airline. You may find that you will have to complete a JOC or a type rating, either of which may be at your own expense, before being offered a contract. The reason for this is to reduce the risk to the airline and to use the qualification as part of the selection process.

I did the JOC at a nominated flight training organization and thoroughly enjoyed the course. It really gave me a taste for flying a jet in an airline environment, and it taught me a lot of practical matters that otherwise I might not have considered. A JOC is likely to consist of the following:

- Crew resource management (CRM)
- Use of the standard operating procedures (SOP) of the sponsoring airline
- Full flight and pre-flight flight-deck preparation
- General handling of a jet
- Raw-data instrument flying
- Use of flight director and autopilot
- Multi-crew co-operation
- Briefings
- Taxiing
- Flight management (dealing with ground crew, ATC, cabin crew, company and the passengers)
- Use of airways plates, SIDs and STARs
- Calculation of aircraft performance
- Dealing with systems failures and use of the quick-reference handbook (QRH)
- Engine failures and fires (on the runway, after take-off, in the cruise and on the approach)
- Missed approaches
- Fuel planning and monitoring
- Planning and flying a full route, taking into consideration all factors of a commercial flight
- Marginal weather operations

The JOC will give you your first significant hands-on experience of flying jet aircraft.

- Route exercises with failures resulting in making a diversion
- Full shut-down procedures
- Final handling test

There is a pass/fail handling test at the end of the course, but if you get through the lessons without any trouble, there is no reason why you should fail the test. Upon successful completion of the JOC or type rating, hopefully you will be offered a contract to work as a first officer for the airline. You may not start immediately, as airlines tend to book and fill courses for type ratings well in advance, so you may have to wait until a course becomes available.

FIRST STEPS AS A FIRST OFFICER

As a new first officer, you can expect to go through an induction course, followed by your type rating. Up to your first line flight, the schedule of training events will be similar to the following:

- Around a week of airline inductions, and emergency and safety training.
- Around two weeks of technical ground school on your aircraft type.
- Around three weeks of flying your aircraft type in a simulator.

- Perhaps the most memorable day of your life – base training. This involves taking your aircraft type up for a short flight without any passengers to practise the take-off and landing.
- Shortly after base training, you will have your first flight 'on-line' with a safety pilot behind you.

It is a good idea to try to get some trips on the flight deck on your days off during training, so that you can observe the procedures in practice and get to know how a line flight operates before you start doing it for yourself.

After a few weeks of flying on-line with a safety pilot behind you, you will take a line check. If you meet the required standard, you will be released on to the line on your own. At last, you will be a fully qualified first officer.

The dream will have come true!

FURTHER READING

Rolls-Royce, *The Jet Engine* (Rolls-Royce, 2005)
An excellent aid to the engine syllabus, this book is full of great diagrams that can help you with the understanding of many engine principles.

Green et al, *Human Factors for Pilots* (Avebury Technical, 1996)
The perfect aid to the human factors syllabus, it looks at many of the areas that you will study during the ATPL syllabus and can therefore help your understanding.

Thom, Trevor, *The Air Pilot's Manual*, Volumes 1–7 (Air Pilot Publisher, 2003)
These books are an excellent aid to any flying training. They are ideal for training for PPL exams and can be used as reference material throughout your ATPL flying training. Amongst other areas, the series covers:

- Aviation Law
- Meteorology
- Navigation
- Principles of Flight
- Flight Instruments
- Aircraft General Knowledge
- Aircraft Performance
- Radio Navigation
- Instrument Flying
- Night Flying
- Human Factors and Limitations
- Radiotelephony

Bruford, David, *To Be A Pilot* (Airlife, 1998)
To Be a Pilot looks at becoming a pilot in a variety of fields, giving information on becoming a private pilot, commercial pilot, airline pilot or a military pilot. It also lists the schools available and current aircraft perators.

Stewart, Stanley, *Flying the Big Jets* (Airlife, 2002)
This book looks at the detail of a large jet aircraft, giving the practicalities of the flying and handling.

Yate, Martin John, *Great Answers to Tough Interview Questions*
(Kogan Page, 2005)
This book is great for inspiring you when it comes to the more tricky interview questions. It also gives lots of advice on how to prepare, what kind of interviews there are, how to present yourself and what to do if it all starts going wrong!

Pelshenke, Paul, *How to Win at Aptitude Tests*
(HarperCollins, 2001)
Gives advice on how to improve your chances at aptitude tests, and gives many example questions to practise.

Shavick, Andrea, *Practice Psychometric Tests*
(How To Books, 2005)
Contains many psychometric tests from the biggest test publisher in the world, SHL Group Plc, which is used by airlines around the world.

Tolley, Harry, and Thomas, Ken, *How to Pass Verbal Reasoning Tests* **(Kogan Page, 2001)**
The only way to improve yourself for the dreaded verbal reasoning test is to practise! This book contains many different types of verbal reasoning questions.

USEFUL ADDRESSES

The Guild of Air Pilots and Air Navigators (GAPAN)
Cobham House
9 Warwick Court
Gray's Inn
London
WC1R 5DJ

www.gapan.org

British Airline Pilots' Association (BALPA)
81 New Road
Harlington
Hayes
Middlesex
UB3 5BG

www.balpa.org

Civil Aviation Authority (CAA)
Aviation House
Gatwick Airport South
West Sussex
RH6 0YR

www.caa.co.uk

Transair Pilot Shop (Pilots' supplies)
Shoreham Airport
Shoreham-by-Sea
West Sussex
BN43 5PA

www.transair.co.uk

Flight Training Europe (ATPL training)
Aeropuerto de Jerez
Base Aerea de La Parra
Jerez de la Frontera
Cadiz
Spain

www.flighttrainingeurope.com

Oxford Aviation (ATPL training)
Kidlington
Oxford
OX5 1QX

www.oxfordaviation.net

Cabair (ATPL training)
Elstree Aerodrome
Borehamwood
Hertfordshire
WD6 3AW

www.cabair.com

INDEX